...nce and a passion for travel.

Rely on Thomas Cook as your travelling companion on your next trip and benefit from our unique heritage.

Thomas Cook **pocket** guides

LEEDS

Your travelling companion since 1873

Thomas Cook

Written by David Cawley

Published by Thomas Cook Publishing
A division of Thomas Cook Tour Operations Limited
Company registration no. 3772199 England
The Thomas Cook Business Park, Unit 9, Coningsby Road,
Peterborough PE3 8SB, United Kingdom
Email: books@thomascook.com, Tel: +44 (0)1733 416477
www.thomascookpublishing.com

Produced by Cambridge Publishing Management Limited
Burr Elm Court, Main Street, Caldecote CB23 7NU
www.cambridgepm.co.uk

ISBN: 978-1-84848-463-4

Cartography supplied by Redmoor Design, Tavistock, Devon

Series Editor: Karen Beaulah
Production/DTP: Steven Collins

Printed and bound in Spain by GraphyCems

CONTENTS

SYMBOLS KEY

The following symbols are used throughout this book:

address telephone website address email
opening times public transport connections important

The following symbols are used on the maps:

information office
hospital
police station
bus station
railway station
church
shopping
airport
POI (point of interest)
city
large town
small town
motorway
main road
minor road
railway
numbers denote featured cafés, restaurants & venues

PRICE CATEGORIES

The ratings below indicate average price rates for a double room per night, including breakfast:
£ under £60 ££ £60–150 £££ over £150
The typical cost for a three-course meal without drinks is as follows:
£ under £20 ££ £20–30 £££ over £30

The Civic Hall owls

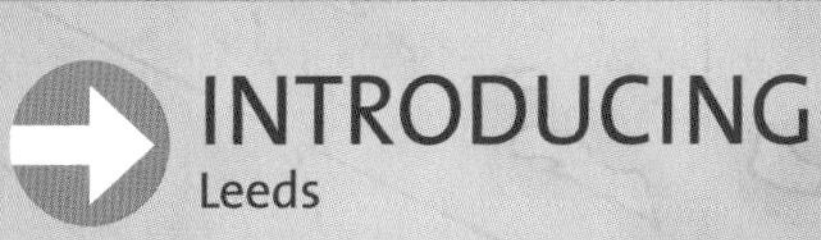

INTRODUCING
Leeds

Introduction

It's cool, it's big and it's one of the friendliest places in the country. Leeds presents visitors with a surprising range of things to do and see. Still bearing the marks of its rich industrial past, buildings that once hummed and throbbed to weaving, printing and engineering now resonate to a different kind of beat. Its watersides have been smartened up to create pleasant places in which to live, work and play, with suits and designer wear replacing overalls and cloth caps as the city transforms itself from manufacturing centre to corporate, legal and banking powerhouse. Mills and warehouses, no longer centres of production, are now fashionable places in which to live or unwind at the end of the working day. Cafés, bars and restaurants have exploded in number recently, and luxury shopping also features heavily in the city's reinvention, attracting people from far and wide to its Victoria Quarter and collection of beautifully preserved shopping arcades. The combination makes Leeds one of the best destinations in the UK for spending hard-earned cash.

This is also an international hub of culture, offering some of the best art and music outside London. A kaleidoscope of festivals is staged in and around the city throughout the year, and theatre lovers will find something different on the bill almost every night. Whether it is opera, ballet, drama, comedy, or the hometown return of pop luminaries Kaiser Chiefs, The Pigeon Detectives or Corinne Bailey Rae, both grand and intimate venues pulsate with a quality, choice and vibrancy hard to find elsewhere.

With all this to offer, it is little wonder that the number of students tempted to Leeds increases with each academic year. The two universities, together with a selection of well-regarded specialist schools and colleges, firmly establishes Yorkshire's biggest city as a renowned seat of learning and research.

A 21st-century city rich in heritage, that enjoys its present, embraces its urban future and is just a short distance from some of the most stunning and unique countryside in the world – the only mystery is why the place doesn't make more of a noise about itself.

Old meets new in Clarence Dock

When to go

SEASONS & CLIMATE

There is no bad time to visit Leeds but, as with all other British cities, spring and summer – when average highs can reach 20°C (68°F) – are the best times to come. Spring is a charming time of year to visit the surrounding Yorkshire Dales, when newborn lambs gambol in the meadows, or in September, when the moorland heather displays its deepest, most vibrant colours. During the winter months the daily temperatures average around 3°C (37°F). Whatever the season, it is wise to carry an umbrella in case of rain.

ANNUAL EVENTS

From hip-hop to opera, indie to brass ensembles, the city's love of music echoes throughout the events calendar. The International Concert Season (Ⓦ www.leedsconcertseason.com) grips the city between October and May, when some of the world's finest musicians from the worlds of jazz, opera, classical and brass congregate to give over 200 performances and features the tri-annual Leeds International Pianoforte competition. Alternatively, the Leeds Festival is an annual rock, indie and dance weekend extravaganza at the end of August featuring global names in each genre (Ⓦ www.leedsfestival.com).

Other sparkling events include the riot of colour, food, music and dance of Leeds Carnival, the oldest West Indian summer carnival in Europe (Ⓦ www.leedscarnival.co.uk) and the Asian Festival (Ⓦ www.leedsasianfestival.com). Leeds Pride (Ⓦ www.leedspride.com) provides gay glamour and fun in early

August, while the stunning backdrop of Kirkstall Abbey hosts a number of events and performances for all ages during the long days of summer (www.leeds.gov.uk/kirkstallabbey) (see page 70). Leeds Shopping Week is an early October celebration for the fashionistas, while the Leeds International Film Festival (www.leedsfilm.com) features premiere screenings and events throughout November. Come December, the city centre embraces the festive spirit with lights, and the German Christkindelmarkt (www.christmasmarkets.com).

Spring blossom in Lovell Park

History

More than anything else, it was sheep that were to be the catalyst for the creation and growth of Leeds. An early Saxon farming community, the earliest known mention of the place name comes in about AD 730, when the Venerable Bede writes of a district known as Loidis, which was located 16 km (10 miles) from the current conurbation. From these humble beginnings both the name and location were to shift gradually: Leodis became Ledes, then Leedes and finally Leeds, and the settlement moved to the banks of the River Aire.

Referred to (as Ledes) in the 1086 Domesday Book, it was to be another six centuries before the city was really to take shape around the church of St Peter and Briggate, 'the road leading to the bridge'. With a population of a then sizeable ten thousand

'LOINERS'

Natives of the city are known as 'Loiners', but the derivation of this name is unclear. One theory is that the term stems from the city's original name of Loidis. Another suggestion is that it comes from the maze of alleyways and yards tucked away behind Briggate, where men of the town often gathered to catch up on news and chew the fat. During the 19th century the entrances to these were known as 'loins' or 'low-ins', and so those people who were born or lived in that area became known as 'Loiners', a name that then extended to all Leeds residents.

people, the numbers tripled over the next 100 years as Leeds expanded into one of the busiest and most prosperous towns in northern England, trading in good-quality wool and cloth from a thriving cottage industry.

During the Industrial Revolution, with developments in factory production, the arrival of barges along the River Aire and Leeds–Liverpool Canal and the coming of the railways, the population expanded even more. While the vast new working population endured deprivation and danger, the industrialists who employed them enjoyed magnificent wealth; they were to declare their riches and power in the construction of the many grand and ornate civic buildings still standing today. Today the economy is centred around legal, financial and service sectors, reflected in the modern glass and steel buildings that, like the mills and warehouses of the past, are once again defining Leeds.

Clarence Dock at night

Culture

Visiting culture vultures will be kept busy with four notable museums and galleries, the **City Museum**, the **Royal Armouries Museum**, **Leeds Art Gallery** and the **Henry Moore Institute**. All are well respected in their fields and always present rewarding shows that change regularly. Leeds also has a strong pedigree in the performing arts, with a collection of theatres staging premieres and well-loved classics, as well as being home to the highly regarded Opera North, Northern Ballet and Phoenix Dance companies.

There are rock, jazz and classical festivals aplenty, and the multicultural nature of the city also means there is a vibrant festival calendar celebrating a diversity of global cultures and religions (see pages 8–9).

Leeds also has a rich literary lineage and can boast among its associates authors as diverse as Alan Bennett, J R R Tolkien, Arthur Ransome, Barbara Taylor Bradford and Keith Waterhouse.

Beyond the urban spread, Salts Mill is permanent home to a selection of work by local son and world-renowned artist and photographer David Hockney, while Harewood House has a rolling programme of traditional and contemporary art exhibitions (see page 70).

The interior of the Corn Exchange

MAKING THE MOST OF
Leeds

Shopping

The range and variety of shopping is arguably the winning ace up the city's sleeve, and visiting shopaholics may well feel that all their birthdays have come at once. Almost 13 sq km (5 sq miles) of space means not just quantity but quality too, with truly something for every taste and budget.

But it's the high-end retail exclusivity of the **Victoria Quarter** that has made Leeds a byword for luxurious and indulgent retail therapy and is the biggest draw for shoppers from outside the city.

It was well-to-do Victorians who first conceived that the shopping experience should be a pleasurable one, and the legacy of their attitude still continues today in a collection of four beautiful historic arcades, preserved in all their splendid glazed tile, glass and ornate ironwork glory. Once home to medieval butchers and slaughterhouses, these retail palaces now house influential names in designer fashion, accessories,

'DON'T ASK THE PRICE: IT'S A PENNY!'

In 1884 Michael Marks, a Russian-born Polish refugee, opened his Penny Bazaar stall in Kirkgate Market, where everything he sold cost a penny. He gradually set up further market stalls across Yorkshire and Lancashire, and ten years later met Yorkshireman Thomas Spencer; the two men went on to form the global institution Marks & Spencer.

The splendid County Arcade

food and furnishings. The exquisite arcades of Thornton's, County, Cross and Queen's are just one of the reasons why Harvey Nichols decided Leeds should be the first place outside of London to house a store bearing its prestigious name.

Nearby, all the big-name retailers are nestled together along a selection of pedestrian-friendly streets. Furthermore, the beautifully preserved traditional market halls are open throughout the week, bombarding the senses and offering myriad affordable necessities and frivolous knick-knacks, just as Marks & Spencer did in the 19th century (see box). Just around the corner, the streets have become a haven for alternative types in search of independent record and urban fashion shops.

Eating & drinking

Yorkshire food – shaped by the northern European climate – has always tended towards the hearty, warming and filling, with savoury pies a particular staple. Yorkshire pudding (originally served as a dessert) still comes with traditional Sunday roasts and can be the size of a plate and filled with an assortment of warm, savoury stews. Yorkshire ham and locally blended black pudding are often found on the breakfast table, while the white fish and harvested shellfish caught at Whitby are regular features of both casual and refined eateries. Favourite of Wallace and Gromit, the distinctive cheese from nearby Wensleydale is also very much part of a rich local culinary tradition, and is available to buy from its dairy shop deep in

Picknickers enjoying a fine evening at Kirkstall Abbey

the Dales (ⓐ Gayle Lane, Hawes ⓣ 01969 667 664 ⓦ www.wensleydale.co.uk). Other Yorkshire specialities include forced rhubarb from the 'rhubarb triangle' (which now has European protected status), as well as barley and hops for the terrific ales of Ossett, Saltaire and Leeds breweries. More surprisingly, nearby Leventhorpe (ⓦ www.englishwineproducers.com/leventhorpe) has become England's most northerly vineyard and has even been winning wine awards in recent years.

Scattered throughout the city, Indian and Italian food is particularly well represented, with nearby Bradford providing plenty of authentic curry houses. Cafés, bars and restaurants from all four corners of the globe can be found in the city centre, with the fashionable **Calls** district offering a characterful choice of waterside drinking and dining options, and the Financial and Legal Quarter playing host to a collection of slightly grander and more formal venues. Big-name chefs setting up eateries in the city include Raymond Blanc, Anthony Flinn, Paul Heathcote at the Olive Press and Jamie Oliver.

Come the warmer months, café tables and chairs spring up on the pavements for some cosmopolitan alfresco sipping and nibbling. Picnickers can choose from any number of delis, such as Salt's (ⓐ 14 Swinegate ⓦ www.saltsdeli.co.uk), or collect fresh produce from Kirkgate Market before heading into the fresh air, either at **Trevelyan Square** or at **Granary Wharf** in the city centre, or further afield in **Hyde** and **Roundhay** parks or **Kirkstall Abbey** for some green open spaces. A picnic among the splendours of the Dales, is tranquillity on a plate, and the traditional country pubs provide exceedingly good food and drink.

Entertainment

For over two centuries Leeds has had a vibrant entertainment scene. From the bygone theatre and music hall tradition, showcased in the hit TV series *The Good Old Days*, which was filmed live at Leeds City Varieties Music Hall and ran from 1953 to 1983, the city has maintained its theatre heritage; it is particularly strong when it comes to drama, dance and opera productions. This, combined with a selection of mainstream cinema venues and the glorious **Hyde Park Picture House** with its art house presentations (see page 78) and a swathe of festivals, including the illustrious six-month **Leeds International Concert Season**, means the city is constantly entertaining its residents and guests.

Regarded as one of the most vibrant and diverse places in the UK to enjoy some 'downtime', buzzing Leeds offers something for everyone, especially those after lively nightlife. At weekends it attracts revellers from surrounding towns and villages, looking for a good night out. Intimate clubs offer an array of 'underground' music, while large and brash super-clubs play the best in pop and cheese. Leeds, having spawned some of the best bands around, attracts them too, and there is no shortage of venues.

Tickets for all performances can be bought directly from venue box offices, from the Leeds Visitor Centre at the railway station, or via its website (ⓦ www.visitleeds.co.uk). For rock gigs, Crash Records (ⓐ 35 The Headrow ⓣ 0113 243 6743 ⓦ www.crashrecords.co.uk) and Jumbo Records (ⓐ 5–6 St Johns Centre ⓣ 0113 245 5570 ⓦ www.jumborecords.co.uk) are a good bet – and both have a ticket desk. *The Leeds Guide* publishes a fortnightly lifestyle and listings magazine (www.leedsguide.co.uk) and is available from most newsagents.

Leeds Town Hall holds numerous concerts

Sport & relaxation

Football, world-class rugby and cricket are all supported with pride, passion and knowledge, while 'horsey' folk will enjoy the nearby Bramham International Horse Trials (a Bramham Park, Wetherby t 01937 846 005 w www.bramham-horse.co.uk Bus: 770). The plethora of racecourses in Yorkshire (w www.goracing.co.uk) are also witness to the area's dedication to equine pursuits.

Lying on the doorstep of some of Britain's most stunningly scenic landscapes, mountain bikers will find over 900 km (560 miles) of varied trails (w www.mtbthedales.org.uk), while walkers, climbers and horse riders can opt for any number of routes. Information can be found at the Yorkshire Dales National Park Authority (t 0300 456 0030 w www.yorkshiredales.org.uk).

SPECTATOR SPORTS

Football

Leeds United FC a Elland Road t 0871 334 1992 w www.leedsunited.com Bus: 1, 51, 55

Horse racing

Wetherby Racecourse. a The Racecourse, York Road, t 01937 582 035 w www.wetherbyracing.co.uk Bus: 770 (10-minute walk from Wetherby Bus Station)

Rugby league & union

Leeds Rhinos play at a Headingley Carnegie Stadium, Headingley t 0871 423 1315 w www.leedsrugby.com Bus: 18,

18A, 56; Train: Headingley or Burley Park (15-minute walk), along with **Leeds Carnegie** As above 0844 248 6651 www.leedscarnegie.co.uk

Cricket

Yorkshire County Cricket Club This illustrious club was founded in 1863. Headingley Carnegie Stadium, Headingley 0871 971 1222 www.yorkshireccc.com Bus: 18, 18A, 56; Train: Headingley or Burley Park (15-minute walk)

PARTICIPATION SPORTS

Golf

City Golf Perfect for hackers and low handicaps on a budget. Kirkstall Road 0113 263 3030 www.citygolfleeds.co.uk Bus: 33, 49

Golf Café Bar Electronically simulated indoor comfort for those short on time and clubs. Granary Wharf 0113 244 4428 www.indoorgolfcafebarleeds.co.uk

Moortown Golf Club Championship course at the quality end of the golfing spectrum and budget. Harrogate Road, Alwoodley 0113 268 6521 www.moortown-gc.co.uk Bus: 36, 71

Adventure sports

Xscape A plethora of pulsating indoor activities for all ages, including winter sports fun and tuition. Colorado Way, Castleford 0871 200 3221 www.xscape.co.uk Train: Glasshoughton

Accommodation

The past few years have seen an explosion in the number of hotels shooting up in the city and there's a place to suit almost every taste and budget. Choices among the familiar large modern and budget hotel chains are plentiful, while the increasing demand for boutique accommodation and serviced apartments has been met with a number of centrally located options. One notable absence is hostel accommodation, though Leeds Metropolitan University does offer cheap accommodation in its halls of residence during the summer (e accommodation@leedsmet.ac.uk). In the surrounding suburbs and just 20 minutes away on public transport, budget hotels, B&Bs and pub accommodation are plentiful, while further into beautiful rural Yorkshire, grand country house hotels, small welcoming inns, guesthouses and campsites set among picturesque Dale villages offer a different reward. Given that the city is a popular business destination, weekends (especially when the events calendar is at its quietest) are the best time to secure some good deals on rates. Booking in advance is always recommended, but should you find yourself arriving without a reservation, the **Leeds Visitor Centre** (a Leeds City Train Station t 0113 242 5242 w www.visitleeds.co.uk) will be happy to help secure you a bed.

HOTELS

Discovery Inn Hotel £ Popular with weekend revellers and part of the Comfort Inn franchise, this centrally located hotel offers budget accommodation on the doorstep of the railway station and nearby nightlife. ⓐ 15 Bishopgate Street ⓣ 0113 242 2555 ⓦ www.comfortinnleeds.co.uk

Holiday Inn Express Leeds Armouries **£** Modern five-storey hotel featuring simply furnished rooms in bright contemporary colours, located in the tranquillity of Clarence Dock and next to the Royal Armouries Museum and conference centre. The city centre is just a ten-minute walk away. ⓐ Armouries Drive, Clarence Dock ⓣ 0870 890 0455 ⓦ www.hiexpressleeds.co.uk

Britannia Hotel Leeds Bradford Airport **££** Set in its own grounds among some lovely Yorkshire countryside, this modern hotel is just 3 km (1¾ miles) from the airport and comes with a pool and health club (small charge), free Wi-Fi, plus airport transfers. ⓐ Leeds Road, Bramhope ⓣ 0871 222 0027 ⓦ www.britanniahotels.com

The view from the City Inn

City Inn Leeds ££ A stylish, friendly hotel on the banks of the river, just a short walk from the station and city centre. State-of-the-art rooms, a choice of eateries, a leisure club and 13th-floor cocktail bar make this a popular place to stay. ⓐ Granary Wharf ⓣ 0113 241 1000 ⓦ www.cityinn.com/leeds

The Met ££ Located in the Financial and Legal Quarter, the ornate listed terracotta façade reveals a stylish interior combining Victorian elegance with contemporary fixtures and facilities. ⓐ King Street ⓣ 0113 245 0841 ⓦ www.methotelleeds.co.uk

Radisson Blu ££ On the northern side of the city centre, this listed building is near the Leeds Art Gallery and City Museum and has been incorporated into The Light entertainment and retail complex. The large and airy Art Deco reception and bar leads to 147 themed rooms. ⓐ The Light, The Headrow ⓣ 0113 236 6100 ⓦ www.radissonblu.co.uk/hotel-leeds

42 The Calls £££ This uniquely crafted waterside hotel is housed in a former corn mill and offers boutique-style accommodation among quirky and artistic surroundings. Bedrooms have been designed around the original mill features within the fashionable Calls district. ⓐ 42 The Calls ⓣ 0113 244 0099 ⓦ www.theetoncollection.com

Quebecs Hotel £££ Set in the former Liberal Club building, this unique boutique hotel offers a grand 19th-century-listed façade wrapped around classic and contemporary luxury, adorned with antiques, wood panelling and vibrant stained-glass windows.

Suites are named after popular sweets. ⓐ 9 Quebec Street ⓣ 0113 244 8989 ⓦ www.theetoncollection.com

The Queens £££ This landmark 1930s Art Deco building in the heart of the city boasts some magnificent examples of the style and period of its day, all beautifully preserved and recently refurbished to reflect its classic grandeur. ⓐ City Square ⓣ 0113 243 5315 ⓦ www.qhotels.co.uk

APARTMENTS

Roomzzz ££ A combination of serviced apartment and boutique hotel, Roomzzz offers modern, designer-led self-catering accommodation with daily housekeeping, 24-hour reception and a complimentary 'Grab & Go' breakfast. Reservations can be made from one night to one year. ⓐ 10 Swinegate ⓣ 0113 233 0400 ⓦ www.roomzzz.co.uk Bus: 117, 202, 203

CAMPING & CARAVANNING

Maustin Caravan Park £ Award-winning conservation site in the heart of verdant *Emmerdale* country, within easy reach of Leeds and Harrogate. Maustin also offers pitches for tents, caravans and holiday homes. ⓐ Wharfe Lane, Kearby ⓣ 0113 288 6234 ⓦ www.maustin.co.uk

Moor Lodge Caravan Park £ Adult-only, tranquil manicured caravan and camping parkland in village setting just 20 minutes from Leeds and well placed for exploring the Dales. ⓐ Blackmoor Lane, Bardsley ⓣ 01937 572 424 ⓦ www.moorlodgecaravanpark.co.uk Bus: 98, X98, 99

THE BEST OF LEEDS

No matter how long your visit, Leeds offers a varied choice of things to do, much of it free and easily accessed. Here are the sights and experiences that you should try not to miss.

TOP 10 ATTRACTIONS

- **Leeds Art Gallery** A renowned collection of some of the best examples of British contemporary art in the UK (see page 47).
- **Leeds Corn Exchange** A celebration of all things culinary within one of Britain's finest examples of Victorian architecture (see page 56).
- **Leeds International Concert Season** The largest of its kind in the UK, including the globally renowned International Pianoforte competition (see page 8).
- **Royal Armouries Museum** An impressive national collection tracing weaponry and armour development and charting its impact to the present day (see page 72).
- **Yorkshire Dales** This stunningly beautiful National Park has inspired some of Britain's best-loved literature, paintings, TV and films (see pages 84–8).

- **Leeds City Museum** A lively and detailed history of the city is provided alongside cultural exhibits collected from around the world (see pages 47–8).

- **Harewood House** This magnificent stately home features a sumptuous collection of art and antiques, manicured gardens and activities for children (see page 70).

- **Thackray Museum** For children and adults alike, this is a lively and innovative exploration of health and medicine of the past, present and future (see page 74).

- **Victoria Quarter** Some of the finest and most elegant shopping in the UK, with over 75 high-end stores in weatherproof surroundings (see pages 14–15).

- **Henry Moore Institute** Beautiful and challenging sculpture presented in stunning surroundings (see page 47).

The magnificent Harewood House

Suggested itineraries

HALF-DAY: LEEDS IN A HURRY

When time is short, head to the City Museum and its eclectic mix of exhibits, which includes insights into the history of the city. Follow this up with a look inside the renowned Leeds Art Gallery for its fine contemporary displays. Both offer visitors a compelling few hours just a short distance from each other.

1 DAY: TIME TO SEE A LITTLE MORE

A full day provides the chance for some serious retail therapy among the high-end splendour of the Victoria Quarter. Briggate is also home to street entertainers and offers a welcome break from plastic transactions. Head next to Kirkgate Market and its dazzling array of sights, sounds and smells, all beneath the ornate market hall ironwork. If shopping is a not for you, make your way instead to the Royal Armouries Museum for some weaponry and armour exploration. Bring the day to a relaxing conclusion with a cocktail and dinner at the architecturally impressive 'foodie' emporium, the Corn Exchange.

2–3 DAYS: SHORT CITY BREAK

In this timeframe, the city can be truly explored. Dwell a little longer in the Leeds Art Gallery and visit the Henry Moore Institute next door. Taking time in between to rest weary limbs in one of the choice of coffee shops, follow the River Aire along a fascinating trail that combines industrial heritage with leisure boats and chic cafés. Alternatively, spend a few hours at the Thackray Museum or journey to neighbouring Bradford for the

National Media Museum and splendid Saltaire Village and Mill. For tranquillity among green spaces, York Gate Gardens or the enormous Roundhay public park both offer an enjoyable respite.

LONGER: ENJOYING LEEDS TO THE FULL

With time of little consequence and having explored the city's attractions, there's a chance to head for sights beyond the city limits. Harewood House features grand stately interiors, fine gardens and wildlife. Leeds is also on the doorstep of some of Britain's finest countryside and its most elegant towns. Harrogate is a study in fine architecture, wide, tree-lined streets and upmarket shopping among colourful and fragrant public parks. In contrast, the Yorkshire Dales is a dramatic landscape of moorland, rolling pasture and evocative ancient villages.

Display cases at the City Museum

Something for nothing

A tired cliché of Yorkshire folk is that they're careful with money; not easily parted with their 'brass'. All nonsense, of course, but when visitors get tired of spending, Leeds does provide a number of welcome free attractions. Most of the museums and galleries in the city are free, but for something a little different head to pedestrianised Briggate to enjoy some street entertainment next to the shopping arcades and market halls. During the International Concert Season, the **Town Hall** plays host to a string of free lunchtime classical concerts, while the rest of the year sees Leeds host a number of festivals and events that require little monetary input (W www.visitleeds.co.uk).

There are a number of engaging trails tracing the city's heritage, including the Owl Trail (W www.leedsowltrail.com) and the waterfront walks (W www.visitleeds.co.uk), which take urban explorers past canal and riverside heritage. Beyond the city limits the **Yorkshire Sculpture Park** (W www.ysp.co.uk) provides aesthetic beauty shaped from a host of materials, while the **Yorkshire Dales** offers expansive nature in all its wild beauty.

YORKSHIRE PASS

The pre-paid Yorkshire Pass offers excellent discounts and provides entry into some of Yorkshire's most popular attractions. The card can be bought online (W www.yorkshirepass.com) or from the Visitor Centre at Leeds City Train Station.

When it rains

As in the rest of Britain, rain is very much a part of life in Leeds. However, during bad and changing weather the city has plenty of attractions to keep visitors amused until the sun comes out again.

The city is awash with indoor retail space – the great beauty of the enchanting Victorian arcades is that they provide complete cover while you browse; the Victoria Quarter houses around 80 major brands from LK Bennett to Louis Vuitton (see pages 14–15).

The Light (see page 49) is a sleek shopping and entertainment complex that offers a 13-screen cinema to accompany its wide range of shops and bars. For a slice of contemporary art, events and more independent cinema screenings, head for **Project Space Leeds** (see page 48).

There's also plenty of culture on offer under dry roofs: **Leeds Art Gallery**, **Leeds City Museum** and the **Royal Armouries Museum** (see pages 47–8, 72) are among the city's principal attractions.

Alternatively, for some spiritual peace and engaging artefacts **Leeds Parish Church** (see pages 56–7) offers tranquillity and fascinating history. **Leeds St Anne's Cathedral** (see pages 48–9), although by no means the largest religious monument in the city, provides welcome contemplative refuge along with daily performances of beautiful choral music.

On arrival

ARRIVING BY AIR, RAIL, ROAD

Leeds shares **Leeds Bradford Airport** (LBA) with the neighbouring city of Bradford and it lies just 13 km (8 miles) north of the city centre. Though relatively small, it does offer a comprehensive choice of national and international routes, though it is dominated by budget and holiday charter airlines (see Directory).

The nearest major international airport is at Manchester (www.manchesterairport.co.uk) and, as an alternative landing point, comes with a 24-hour direct train service to Leeds, which takes 80 minutes.

From Leeds Bradford Airport, the half-hourly **Airlink** bus service (Bus: 757) takes 40-minutes from outside the terminal building to downtown Leeds City Bus Station and the mainline railway station (0113 345 7676 www.wymetro.com).

Alternatively, taxis are available from the terminal building and cost in the region of £20. City Cabs (0113 246 9999 www.citycabsleeds.co.uk) can be hailed there, while mini-cab firms must be booked before or on arrival. The train station's location right in the heart of the city makes it an extremely convenient and green way of travelling to Leeds. Nationwide services are frequent and numerous.

Those coming by car will find the city at the crossroads of the M1 and M62 motorways. Leeds is easy to reach from all points on the compass and, once there, the A64 and A58 inner ring roads whisk traffic into the heart of the city's one-way system. Parking prices vary but a rough guide for weekdays is

£1.80 for the first hour, rising to £8.00 for five hours. Secure overnight parking starts at £12.00. Be aware that the local council is tough on illegal parking. While there is plenty of signage for motorists, the road system can be confusing to newcomers and it is worth bringing a Sat Nav with you. Coach services can take the strain and deliver passengers into the centre from across the UK. Though landlocked, Leeds is just a short 90-minute journey from the ferry ports of Liverpool and Hull for services to Ireland, Holland and Belgium.

FINDING YOUR FEET

Easy to navigate on foot, the city centre is compact and bounded to the west, north and east by the busy inner ring roads, and to the south by the River Aire. West Yorkshire Police (see Directory) has responsibility for tackling crime at a local level. The people of Yorkshire are a friendly and welcoming bunch as a rule and Leeds has no more issues with crime and safety than any other European city. Like any big city, there are pockets of the districts surrounding the centre that offer little reward for tourists and are perhaps best avoided after dark. As always, human instincts and concerns can be quite a reliable indicator, and are always best acted upon.

ORIENTATION

Leeds city centre is pedestrian friendly and most of the streets are traffic free. Albion Street cuts the city in half north to west, while Westgate, The Headrow and Eastgate (all one street) runs through the middle, from west to east. A useful landmark is Leeds University's Parkinson Tower, which is set on the hillside to

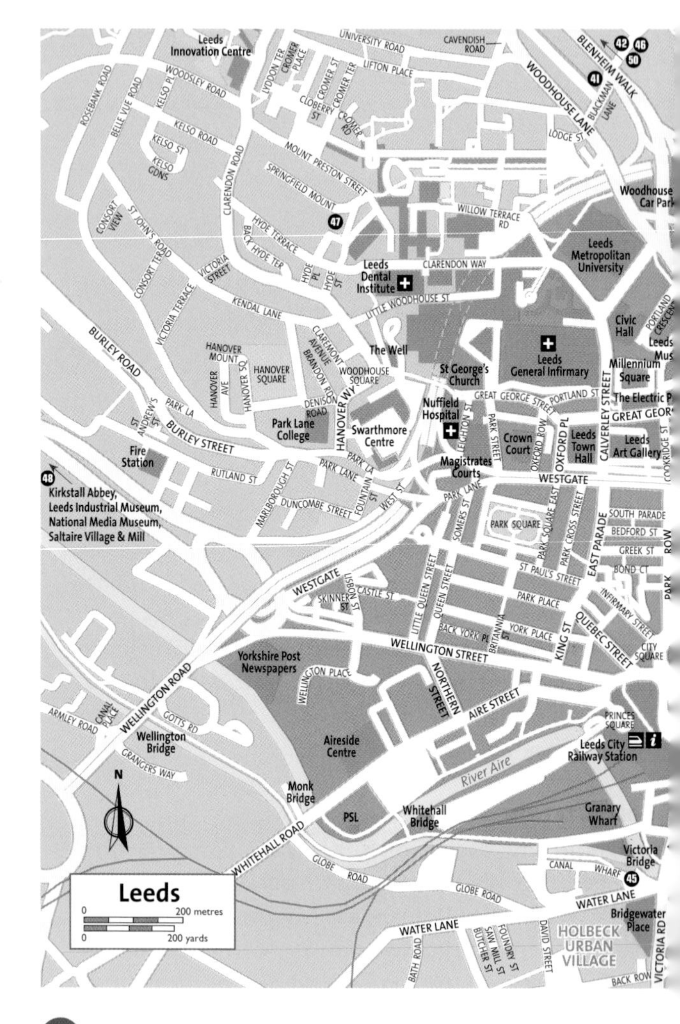
Leeds
0 200 metres
0 200 yards
Leeds Innovation Centre
UNIVERSITY ROAD
CAVENDISH ROAD
BLENHEIM WALK
WOODHOUSE LANE
BLACKMAN LANE
LODGE ST
Woodhouse Car Park
WOODSLEY ROAD
KELSO PL
KELSO ROAD
KELSO ST
KELSO GDNS
ROSEBANK ROAD
BELLE VUE ROAD
LYDDON TER
CROMER PLACE
CROMER ST
CROMER TER
CROMER RD
CLOBERRY ST
LIFTON PLACE
MOUNT PRESTON STREET
SPRINGFIELD MOUNT
CLARENDON ROAD
WILLOW TERRACE RD
CONSORT VIEW
ST JOHN'S ROAD
CONSORT TERR
HYDE TERRACE
BACK HYDE TER
HYDE PL
HYDE ST
VICTORIA STREET
Leeds Dental Institute
CLARENDON WAY
Leeds Metropolitan University
VICTORIA TERRACE
KENDAL LANE
LITTLE WOODHOUSE ST
Civic Hall
PORTLAND CRESCENT
BURLEY ROAD
HANOVER MOUNT
HANOVER SQUARE
HANOVER AVE
HANOVER SQ
CLAREMONT AVENUE
BRANDON RD
The Well
WOODHOUSE SQUARE
St George's Church
Leeds General Infirmary
Millennium Square
The Electric P
GREAT GEORGE STREET
PORTLAND ST
CALVERLEY STREET
GREAT GEOR
ST ANDREW'S ST
PARK LA
DENISON ROAD
HANOVER WY
Park Lane College
Swarthmore Centre
Nuffield Hospital
LEIGHTON ST
PARK STREET
Crown Court
OXFORD ROW
OXFORD PL
Leeds Town Hall
Leeds Art Gallery
COOKRIDGE ST
BURLEY STREET
Fire Station
RUTLAND ST
PARK LA
PARK LANE
Magistrates Courts
WESTGATE
Kirkstall Abbey, Leeds Industrial Museum, National Media Museum, Saltaire Village & Mill
MARLBOROUGH ST
DUNCOMBE STREET
FOUNTAIN ST
WEST ST
PARK LANE
SOMERS ST
PARK SQUARE
PARK SQUARE EAST
PARK CROSS STREET
SOUTH PARADE
BEDFORD ST
GREEK ST
BOND CT
EAST PARADE
PARK ROW
ST PAUL'S STREET
WESTGATE
LISBON ST
CASTLE ST
SKINNER ST
LITTLE QUEEN STREET
QUEEN STREET
PARK PLACE
INFIRMARY STREET
BACK YORK PL
BRITANNIA ST
YORK PLACE
KING ST
QUEBEC STREET
CITY SQUARE
WELLINGTON STREET
Yorkshire Post Newspapers
WELLINGTON PLACE
NORTHERN STREET
AIRE STREET
WELLINGTON ROAD
ARMLEY ROAD
CANAL PLACE
GOTTS RD
Wellington Bridge
GRANGERS WAY
Aireside Centre
PRINCES SQUARE
Leeds City Railway Station
River Aire
N
Monk Bridge
PSL
Whitehall Bridge
Granary Wharf
WHITEHALL ROAD
GLOBE ROAD
GLOBE ROAD
Victoria Bridge
CANAL WHARF
WATER LANE
WATER LANE
Bridgewater Place
BATH ROAD
BUTCHER ST
SAW MILL ST
FOUNDRY ST
DAVID STREET
HOLBECK URBAN VILLAGE
VICTORIA RD
BACK ROW

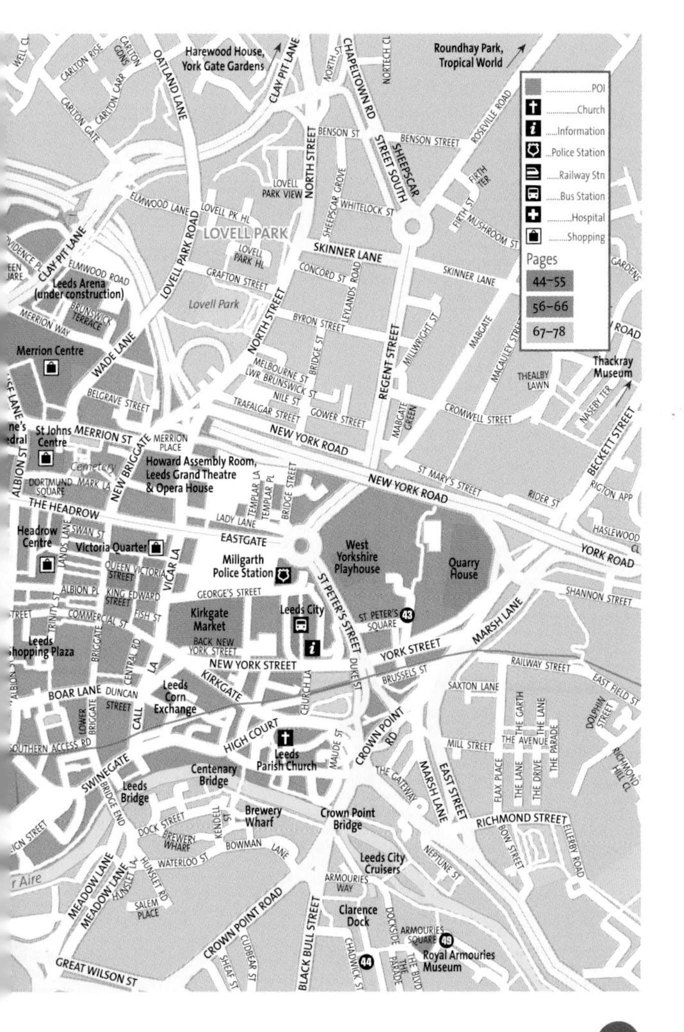

Harewood House, York Gate Gardens
Roundhay Park, Tropical World
POI
Church
Information
Police Station
Railway Stn
Bus Station
Hospital
Shopping
Pages
44–55
56–66
67–78
LOVELL PARK
Lovell Park
Leeds Arena (under construction)
Merrion Centre
St Johns Centre
Cemetery
Howard Assembly Room, Leeds Grand Theatre & Opera House
Headrow Centre
Victoria Quarter
Millgarth Police Station
West Yorkshire Playhouse
Quarry House
Kirkgate Market
Leeds City
Leeds Shopping Plaza
Leeds Corn Exchange
Leeds Parish Church
Centenary Bridge
Leeds Bridge
Brewery Wharf
Crown Point Bridge
Leeds City Cruisers
Clarence Dock
Royal Armouries Museum
Thackray Museum
River Aire
CLAY PIT LANE
OATLAND LANE
CHAPELTOWN RD
NORTH STREET
SHEEPSCAR STREET SOUTH
BENSON STREET
ROSEVILLE ROAD
SKINNER LANE
LOVELL PARK ROAD
ELMWOOD LANE
ELMWOOD ROAD
WADE LANE
MERRION STREET
NEW BRIGGATE
THE HEADROW
EASTGATE
NEW YORK ROAD
REGENT STREET
YORK ROAD
YORK STREET
MARSH LANE
ST PETER'S STREET
KIRKGATE
NEW YORK STREET
BOAR LANE
HIGH COURT
CROWN POINT RD
CROWN POINT ROAD
RICHMOND STREET
EAST STREET
SWINEGATE
MEADOW LANE
BLACK BULL STREET
GREAT WILSON ST

the northwest of the city. Other major landmarks include Leeds station to the south and Kirkgate Market to the east. If you find yourself confronted with either a busy motorway or the River Aire, then you have reached the limits of the city centre. As a rough guide and with the above boundaries in mind, it takes 15 minutes to walk from north to south and from east to west. Walking up a gentle gradient usually means you are walking in a northerly direction.

GETTING AROUND

Given its compact nature, walking is the best way to get around the city centre. Leeds has no underground or tram system and locals rely instead on local buses and trains to get around. For rail routes, times and fares around Leeds and to out-of-town areas, visit Ⓦ www.nationalrail.co.uk. For details on rail passes, see Ⓦ www.northernrail.org

The major bus station for local journeys can be found on New York Street, while the railway station, Boar Lane, Vicar Lane and Infirmary Street also have sizeable bus interchanges as well as numerous bus stops in between. All provide route information on their signs. Local bus travel protocol is the same as in the rest of the UK. As the bus approaches the bus stop, raise an arm to signal that you want the driver to pick you up, and on boarding state your destination and what type of ticket you need (single, return, day pass etc.). Buses use cash only and the correct change is generally appreciated.

For a range of unlimited day and seasonal bus travel passes, ask the bus driver or visit the Travel Centre within the Leeds City Bus Station on New York Street.

It takes just 15 minutes to walk across the city

FREECITYBUS
The Freecitybus provides fully accessible free bus travel around key spots in the city centre and into the university district and runs every few minutes.

For information on getting around the city, including routes, times and passes, contact West Yorkshire Metro. ⓣ 0113 245 7676 ⓦ www.wymetro.com ◷ 06.30–19.30 Mon–Sat, closed Sun

Taxis

Taxi ranks are plentiful and, obvious from their distinctive black and white livery, the traditional hackney and saloon cars of City Cabs can be hailed on the street (see page 32).

Cycling

Those arriving with bicycles or with cycling in mind will find that the city lies on a gentle gradient leading northwards up from the River Aire towards the hospital and university districts. Traffic is kept to a minimum in the heart of the city and there are numerous dedicated cycle lanes and places to securely lock bikes, including at the train and bus stations. For students at the universities, a low-cost bike-hire scheme that offers all kinds of equipment and services on production of student ID is available throughout term-time. See ⓦ www.leeds.ac.uk/velocampus

For up-to-the-minute information on public transport and car parking in and around the centre of Leeds, contact Leeds Travel. ⓣ 0113 242 5242 ⓦ www.leedstravel.info

A cyclist on the towpath in Leeds

JOIN THE CLUB

One alternative to standard car hire is to join a car club scheme. Leeds City Council has endorsed such a project and, for an annual fee of £50, eco-friendly vehicles can be rented by the hour, day or longer from a choice of locations in the city centre and selective suburbs.
ⓣ 0113 350 3930 ⓦ www.citycarclub.co.uk
ⓔ leeds@citycarclub.co.uk

CAR HIRE

Hiring a car to navigate the compact city centre is unnecessary; however, if public transport isn't practical, renting a car might be considered for getting out into the surrounding countryside. Costs and terms do vary, but a rough figure for one day's rental on a medium-sized car should be between £45 and £55. (If you are planning to hire a car, remember to bring two domestic utility bills as proof of address, along with all parts of your driving licence.)

Leeds Town Hall in high summer

THE CITY OF
Leeds

Introduction to city areas

Using nature and town planning as boundaries, the city has been divided into three easily distinctive areas. **West of Albion Street** contains the bulk of grand buildings, museums, galleries and public squares, and is home to some of the swankiest hotels and restaurants. **East of Albion Street** is the oldest part of the city, which now plays host to most of its retail and entertainment attractions, including the stunning arcades in the **Victoria Quarter**, most of the theatres and the waterside **Calls** district, with its thriving restaurant and bar scene.

Encasing the city centre, a whole gamut of differing landscapes can be explored and enjoyed. From rolling hills to heritage-rich **Bradford** and **Saltaire**; and from trendy leafy suburbs to new glass and steel structures along the southern banks of the River Aire. All of the city's major sporting venues are here, as well as the big stately homes and public parks, and local public transport gets you there with ease.

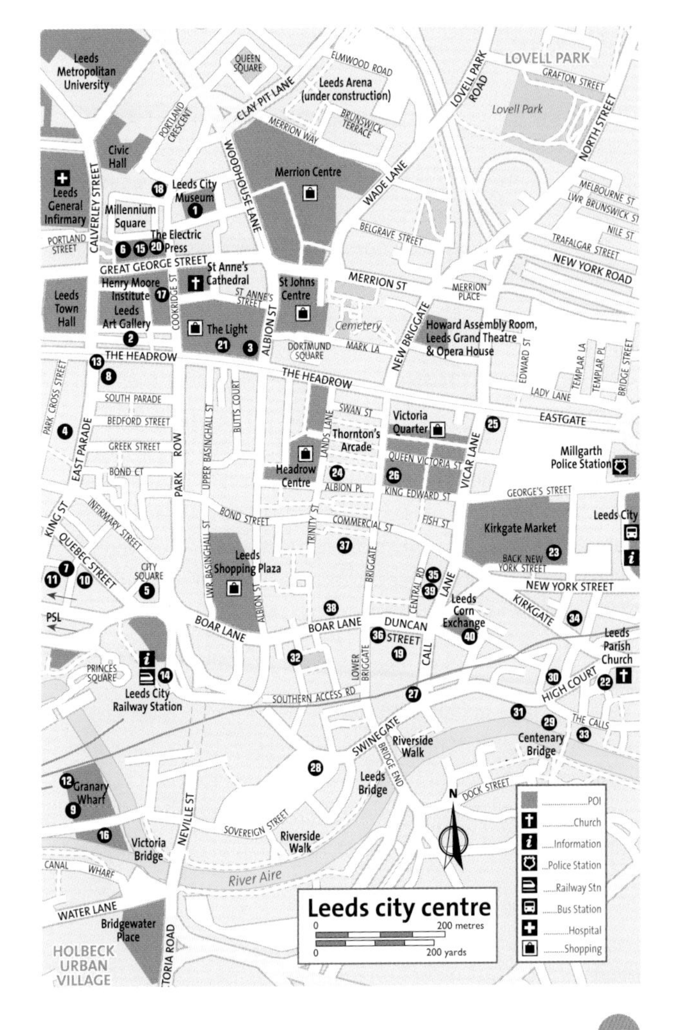
Leeds city centre
0
200 metres
0
200 yards
POI
Church
Information
Police Station
Railway Stn
Bus Station
Hospital
Shopping
Leeds Metropolitan University
QUEEN SQUARE
ELMWOOD ROAD
LOVELL PARK
GRAFTON STREET
Lovell Park
LOVELL PARK ROAD
CLAY PIT LANE
Leeds Arena (under construction)
MERRION WAY
BRUNSWICK TERRACE
PORTLAND CRESCENT
Civic Hall
WOODHOUSE LANE
Merrion Centre
WADE LANE
NORTH STREET
MELBOURNE ST
LWR BRUNSWICK ST
NILE ST
Leeds General Infirmary
CALVERLEY STREET
Leeds City Museum
Millennium Square
BELGRAVE STREET
TRAFALGAR STREET
NEW YORK ROAD
PORTLAND STREET
The Electric Press
GREAT GEORGE STREET
St Anne's Cathedral
St Johns Centre
MERRION ST
MERRION PLACE
Henry Moore Institute
Leeds Town Hall
Leeds Art Gallery
COOKRIDGE ST
ST ANNE'S STREET
The Light
ALBION ST
Cemetery
NEW BRIGGATE
Howard Assembly Room, Leeds Grand Theatre & Opera House
DORTMUND SQUARE
MARK LA
EDWARD ST
TEMPLAR LA
TEMPLAR PL
BRIDGE STREET
THE HEADROW
PARK CROSS STREET
SOUTH PARADE
BUTTS COURT
SWAN ST
LADY LANE
EASTGATE
BEDFORD STREET
UPPER BASINGHALL ST
Victoria Quarter
Thornton's Arcade
LANDS LANE
GREEK STREET
ROW
QUEEN VICTORIA ST
VICAR LANE
Millgarth Police Station
EAST PARADE
BOND CT
PARK
Headrow Centre
ALBION PL
KING EDWARD ST
GEORGE'S STREET
KING ST
INFIRMARY STREET
BOND STREET
TRINITY ST
COMMERCIAL ST
FISH ST
Kirkgate Market
Leeds City
QUEBEC STREET
CITY SQUARE
LWR BASINGHALL ST
Leeds Shopping Plaza
BRIGGATE
CENTRAL RD
LANE
BACK NEW YORK STREET
NEW YORK STREET
ALBION ST
Leeds Corn Exchange
KIRKGATE
PSL
BOAR LANE
BOAR LANE
DUNCAN STREET
CALL
Leeds Parish Church
PRINCES SQUARE
Leeds City Railway Station
LOWER BRIGGATE
HIGH COURT
SOUTHERN ACCESS RD
THE CALLS
SWINEGATE
Riverside Walk
Centenary Bridge
BRIDGE END
Granary Wharf
Leeds Bridge
DOCK STREET
NEVILLE ST
N
SOVEREIGN STREET
Riverside Walk
Victoria Bridge
CANAL WHARF
River Aire
WATER LANE
Bridgewater Place
HOLBECK URBAN VILLAGE
TORIA ROAD

City centre west

The railway station is where most people arriving in Leeds will get their first glimpse of the city. Buses and taxis queue outside, though – like the rest of the centre – it's all managed relatively easily on foot, with the majority of attractions no more than a 15-minute walk away. This area is dominated by the Financial and Legal Quarter, with the Civic Quarter and its limits defined by Albion Street to the east and the River Aire to the south.

SIGHTS & ATTRACTIONS

City Square

Gateway from the station to the Financial and Legal Quarter, the pedestrian square features fountains and a collection of statues depicting local worthies, nymphs and, as its centrepiece, a statue of the Black Prince on horseback, all in the shadow of the grandiose former Post Office. Bus: Freecitybus

Civic Hall

Opened in 1933 as home to the city council, this is now host to a number of civic and performance events. As well as some fine Romanesque columns, the white stone exterior is also home to two giant golden owls, the official symbol of Leeds. ⓐ Millennium Square ⓣ 0113 234 8080 Bus: Freecitybus

The Electric Press

This former Victorian carriage manufacturer is now home to an enclosed atrium of bars and restaurants, plus the

The Black Prince statue in the City Square

Carriageworks theatre (see page 55). 14 Great George Street
0784 984 2892 www.electricpressuk.com
Bus: Freecitybus

Granary Wharf

Former loading and administration basin for the Leeds and Liverpool canal, Granary Wharf offers both industrial heritage and a collection of swish hotels, bars and restaurants on its scrubbed-up cobbled banks. This is a good place to watch the colourful traditional narrow boats pass through the two locks.
Dark Neville Street, Neville Street

Leeds Town Hall

Opened by Queen Victoria, this landmark building in the heart of the Civic Quarter was another statement of the wealth and power of industrial Leeds in the 19th century. Along with its day-to-day civic functions, it is also one of the venues used during the Leeds International Concert Season (see page 8).

Millennium Square

This large public space was opened by Nelson Mandela at the turn of the century and is flanked by a collection of prime Victorian civic buildings. It is a focal point for a number of concerts, outdoor theatre events, street entertainment and markets, as well as one of Europe's largest ice-skating rinks. Major sport events are also broadcast here via a giant screen.
Daily (Jan–Mar) Admission charge to rink and some events

Civic Hall from Millennium Square

CULTURE

Henry Moore Institute

Endowed by local boy Henry Moore, the institute is a rewarding discovery of sculpture, both ancient and modern, supported by ever-changing exhibitions, talks and events. ⓐ The Headrow ⓣ 0113 246 7467 ⓦ www.henry-moore.org ⓞ 10.00–17.30 daily, closed bank holidays ⓝ Bus: Freecitybus

Leeds Art Gallery

Built in 1888, this fine example of the city's civic pride is a popular meeting place for locals on its raised frontage overlooking the centre's main thoroughfare. This is one of the best permanent and touring collections of modern, contemporary and new media in the UK and includes esteemed works from the likes of Barbara Hepworth, Antony Gormley and Francis Bacon.
ⓐ The Headrow ⓣ 0113 247 8256 ⓦ www.leeds.gov.uk/artgallery
ⓞ 10.00–17.00 Mon, Tues & Thur–Sat, 12.00–17.00 Wed, 13.00–17.00 Sun, closed bank holidays ⓝ Bus: Freecitybus

Leeds City Museum

Formerly known as the Leeds Institute, this grand 19th-century edifice was built in the classical style to educate and entertain city workers. It is now a manageable museum for adults and children spread over three floors and featuring engaging galleries of the ancients, including the 'Leeds Mummy', along with lively natural history displays and a floor dedicated to telling the fascinating history of Leeds through to the present day. ⓐ Millennium Square ⓣ 0113 224 3732

OUTDOOR REFRESHMENT

For outdoor refreshment deep in the Financial and Legal Quarter, Park Square offers a green oasis and a pleasant place to relax with a picnic or coffee among the suits, birdsong and fine Georgian architecture. Nearby St Paul's Street offers a choice of quality cafés and takeaways such as the Sesame Café (w www.ilovesesame.co.uk) with its pleasing mix of sushi and pies.

w www.leeds.gov.uk/citymuseum 10.00–17.00 Tues, Wed & Fri, 10.00–19.00 Thur, 11.00–17.00 Sat & Sun, closed Mon except bank holidays Bus: Freecitybus

PSL

Just a five-minute walk from the train station, Project Space Leeds is an independent, artist-led gallery featuring excellent modern and contemporary art by local, national and international artists. a Whitehall Waterfront, 2 Riverside Way t 0793 023 6383 w www.projectspaceleeds.org.uk 12.00–17.00 Wed–Sat during exhibition times only

St Anne's Cathedral

Opening its doors in 1904, this is one of the most celebrated churches of the Arts and Crafts movement. Famous also for its liturgical music, it maintains this strong heritage today with beautiful choral performances throughout the week. a Great George Street t 0113 245 4545 w www.leedscathedral.org.uk

Choral: Sun–Fri; ring or check website for details
Bus: Freecitybus

RETAIL THERAPY

Shopaholics will mostly satisfy their cravings in the eastern area of the city. However, the western end does have its rewards, including the branded clothing and accessories stores of **The Light** shopping and entertainment centre (The Headrow 0113 218 2060 www.thelightleeds.co.uk Bus: Freecitybus). For all that's brand familiar on numerous other high streets across the land, the enclosed **Leeds Shopping Plaza** and open Bond Street and Albion Street are the places to head for traffic-free retail satisfaction. The Financial and Legal Quarter is home to a fine collection of bespoke clothing and footwear retailers, ideal for visitors wanting attire for formal occasions or who have arrived on business and been caught on the hop.
These include **Craggs** (161 The Headrow 0113 246 8181 www.craggsshoesonline.com) and **James Ashley** (12 St Paul's Street 0113 244 5329).

TAKING A BREAK

Cafés

Leeds City Museum Café £ ❶ Bright and spacious terraced café astride Millennium Square. Salads, sandwiches, award-winning pies and local speciality cakes can be washed down with traditional cordials and Fairtrade coffee and tea. Millennium Square 0113 263 7915 11.00–18.00 Tues–Sun, closed Mon

Tiled Hall £ ❷ Large vaulted ceilings above stunningly ornate glazed tiling make this a gem of a place for coffee, cake, salads, savoury pies and sandwiches. ⓐ Leeds Art Gallery, The Headrow ⓣ 0113 224 4811 ⓦ www.tiledhallcafe.co.uk ⓛ 09.00–20.00 Mon–Wed, 09.00–17.00 Thur & Fri, 10.00–17.00 Sat, 13.00–17.00 Sun

Restaurants

Browns Bar & Brasserie £ ❸ The grand marble and wood rooms of this former banking hall belie the affordability of this eatery. British and European food is the theme of choice for this national chain and there are always good deals to be had on their ever-changing set menus. Close to the Vue cinemas (see page 55). ⓐ The Light, The Headrow ⓣ 0113 243 9353 ⓦ www.browns-restaurants.co.uk ⓛ 12.00–22.00 daily

Gourmet Burger Kitchen £ ❹ Does exactly what it says on the door, though with arguably more flair and finesse than the standard burger chains. ⓐ 29 East Parade ⓣ 0113 243 5866 ⓦ www.gbk.co.uk ⓛ 12.00–23.00 Mon–Sat, 11.00–22.00 Sun

Chino Latino ££ ❺ Highly regarded fusion restaurant blending Far Eastern cuisine with a dash of South American spice – all served up in dark, contemporary surroundings. Tasting, bar platters and à la carte menus to suit all levels of appetite and budget. ⓐ Boar Lane, City Square ⓣ 0113 380 4080 ⓦ www.chinolatino.co.uk ⓛ 18.00–22.30 daily

Ha Ha Bar & Grill ££ ❻ National chain specialising in casual classic British food shares menu space with predominantly Mediterranean offerings, all within the restored and now cool industrial interiors of a former carriage factory. The bar design is a sight to behold, and in warmer weather there is a large terrace set on Millennium Square. ⓐ The Electric Press ⓣ 0113 244 8835 ⓦ www.hahaonline.co.uk ◔ 10.00–22.00 daily

Mio Modo ££ ❼ Art and food join forces in this friendly and stylish restaurant. Well-cooked Italian staples compete with a large choice of fish and meat dishes presented with panache and accompanied by an affordable wine list. ⓐ 2–4 Britannia Street ⓣ 0113 242 6655 ⓦ www.miomodo.co.uk ◔ 18.00–22.30 Mon–Fri, 18.00–23.00 Sat, closed Sun

Sam's Chop House ££ ❽ Award-winning food and drinks served in an atmosphere reminiscent of a gentleman's club. The corned-beef hash is legendary and there is live jazz every Sunday afternoon. ⓐ 8 South Parade ⓣ 0113 204 2490 ⓦ www.samschophouse.co.uk ◔ 12.00–21.30 Mon–Sat, 12.00–17.00 Sun

Wasabi Teppan-Yaki ££ ❾ Dining for all ages in bright, friendly surroundings beneath the railway station. Go for the teppanyaki table, where your food is cooked by the chefs as you watch, or for light appetites or lunch, opt for the noodle bar or one of the sashimi or sushi combination platters. ⓐ Dark Neville Street ⓣ 0113 245 1856 ⓦ www.wasabiteppanyaki.co.uk ◔ 18.00–23.00 Mon, 12.00–14.30 & 18.00–23.00 Tues–Sat, 13.00–20.00 Sun

The Old Post Office, now a popular seafood restaurant

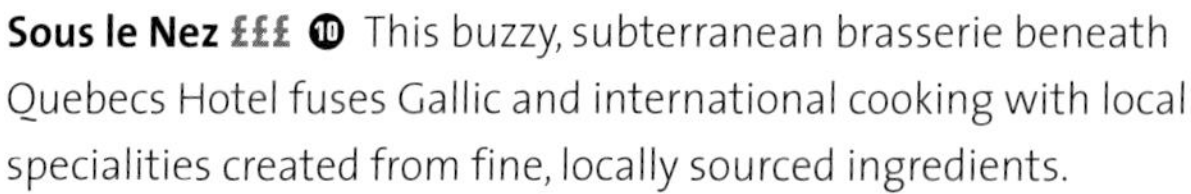

Sous le Nez £££ ❿ This buzzy, subterranean brasserie beneath Quebecs Hotel fuses Gallic and international cooking with local specialities created from fine, locally sourced ingredients. ⓐ Quebec House, Quebec Street ⓣ 0113 244 0108 ⓦ www.souslenez.com 🕒 12.00–14.30 & 18.00–22.00 Mon–Fri, 12.00–14.00 & 18.00–23.00 Sat, closed Sun & bank holidays

AFTER DARK

Pubs & bars

Baby Jupiter £ ⓫ An affectionate nod to the 60s and 70s, ably supported by a creative playlist aimed at a knowledgeable and friendly crowd. ⓐ 11 York Place ⓣ 0113 242 1202

The Hop £ ⓬ Set beneath the arches of the city's railway station, this vaulted bar specialises in local beers and live music. Rock idol murals and seminal album-cover wallpaper adorn the upstairs walls and ceiling. ⓐ City Inn, Granary Wharf

Mr Foley's £ ⓭ This friendly bar, tucked inside a Grade-II-listed building, appeals to a mixed clientele and features traditional real ales and a vast array of imported beers that can be enjoyed from the comfort of leather sofas. Sports fans can watch live events on big-screen TVs. ⓐ 159 The Headrow ⓣ 0113 242 9674

Scarborough Hotel £ ⓮ This ornate Victorian pub opposite the railway station is popular with the real-ale crowd, who also tuck into its large selection of tasty pies. It's boisterous, to say the least, on football match days. ⓐ Bishopgate Street ⓣ 0113 243 4590

Local lad Henry Moore is well represented in the city

Epernay ££ ⑮ One of the few dedicated champagne bars in Leeds, offering choices from 21 different 'houses' as well as an extensive cocktail list – all among the stylish industrial chic surroundings of The Electric Press complex. ⓐ The Electric Press, 12 Great George Street ⓣ 0113 242 9977 ⓦ www.epernaychampagnebars.com

Skylounge ££ ⑯ Star spotting in every sense. This chic, minimalist cocktail bar attracts local celebs and sporting heroes to its 13th-floor with its 360-degree panoramic views of the city and night sky. Hotel prices, but well worth it for the matchless views. ⓐ City Inn, Granary Wharf ⓣ 0113 243 8885 ⓦ www.cityinn.com/leeds

Clubs & venues

Nation of Shopkeepers ⓱ An eminent live music bar specialising predominantly in indie rock and variations on that theme. Inside, it's decorated in an array of memorabilia and locally commissioned artwork, while its exterior is also worth a look. ⓐ 27–37 Cookridge Street ⓦ www.anationofshopkeepers.com

O2 Academy ⓲ Large live-music venue with a full diary of big-name music stars and up-and-coming talent. Tickets available from the box office. ⓐ 55 Cookridge Street ⓣ 0113 389 1555 ⓦ www.o2academyleeds.co.uk

The Space ⓳ Pop culture decoration meets house, soul and electro tunes on the dance floor. Global guest DJs and special events ensure this well-established city favourite keeps you dancing into the wee small hours. ⓐ Hurst Yard, Duncan Street ⓣ 0113 246 1030 ⓦ www.thespaceleeds.com

Theatre & cinema

The Carriageworks ⓴ A thriving 350-seat theatre supporting new and challenging performance art, comedy and drama. ⓐ The Electric Press, 3 Millennium Square ⓣ 0113 224 3801 ⓦ www.carriageworkstheatre.org.uk

The Vue ㉑ A 13-screen multiplex cinema in the heart of The Light retail and entertainment complex. ⓐ The Light, The Headrow ⓣ 0871 224 0240 ⓦ www.myvue.com

City centre east

East of the railway station, no more than ten minutes' walk from the heart of the city, lie most of the shopping, theatres and buzzing nightlife, in and around The Calls district of Leeds. The area is bounded by Albion Street in the west and by the River Aire in the south, and lies to the south and west of the ring road.

SIGHTS & ATTRACTIONS

Kirkgate Market

The vast and vibrant halls of Kirkgate Market show off their beautiful façade on Vicar Lane and contain some wonderfully ornate decoration within (see pages 59, 60).

Leeds Corn Exchange

One of the finest examples of Victorian architecture in the country, this grand, circular, domed building is now home to restaurateur Anthony Flinn's growing empire of eateries. It was restored in 2008 and, though still slightly bereft of general traders in its gloriously ornate space, foodies will still find plenty to enjoy. ⓐ 42 Call Lane ⓣ 0113 234 0363 ⓦ www.cornx.net ◷ 09.00–18.00 Mon–Sat, 11.00–16.00 Sun ⓝ Bus: Freecitybus

Leeds Parish Church

St Peter's is the largest church in the city and has a number of interesting historical features, including within the decorated sanctuary area the famous 10th-century Leeds Cross. ⓐ Kirkgate

0113 243 9731 www.leedsparishchurch.org.uk 08.30–15.00 Mon–Fri, 09.00–14.00 Sat Bus: Freecitybus (stop on the corner of Kirkgate and New Market Street)

Thornton's Arcade

The ornate 'Ivanhoe' clock located above the western entrance features an animatronics collection of colourful characters taken from Sir Walter Scott's novel of the same name. Arrive on the quarter of each hour during shopping hours to watch the performance. Thornton's Arcade, Lands Lane

Waterfront walks

Once people tried to flee the area surrounding the River Aire and Leeds–Liverpool Canal, now people can't get enough of it;

The famous 'Ivanhoe' clock in Thornton's Arcade

the banks are packed with refurbished warehouses and newly built apartments, bars and restaurants. The stretch from Granary Wharf to Crown Point Bridge is well worth a look and includes the redeveloped Brewery Wharf and Clarence Dock.

CULTURE

Theatres

Howard Assembly Room

Located in the Grand Theatre and overseen by Opera North, this contemporary arena offers a repertoire of newly commissioned and traditional performing arts. ⓐ 46 New Briggate ⓣ 0844 848 2727 ⓦ www.howardassemblyroom.co.uk ⓡ Bus: Freecitybus, 4, 35, 71

Narrowboats in Clarence Dock

Leeds Grand Theatre & Opera House

As well as being home to the locally based Northern Ballet (ⓦ www.northernballettheatre.co.uk) and Opera North (ⓦ www.operanorth.co.uk), the Grand hosts heavyweight touring productions like the ENO, Rambert Dance Company and Royal Shakespeare Co. ⓐ 46 New Briggate ⓣ 0844 848 2706 ⓦ www.leedsgrandtheatre.com Bus: Freecitybus, 4, 35, 71

RETAIL THERAPY

A spender's paradise, Leeds offers some of the best shopping to be found anywhere in the UK. The retail areas are chiefly concentrated in the eastern part of the city centre. Almost all of the shopping streets are traffic free and enclosed against the elements, and have a diversity that makes even just browsing a pleasure. Probably best known are the collection of four beautifully preserved Victorian arcades – **County**, **Cross**, **Queen's** and **Thornton's** – all situated in the aptly named Victoria Quarter (ⓦ www.v-q.co.uk). Often referred to as the 'Knightsbridge of the North', this is about as high end a shopping experience as you are likely to get, and it's little wonder that **Harvey Nichols** (ⓐ 107–111 Briggate ⓣ 0113 204 8888 ⓦ www.harveynichols.com) chose Leeds as the setting for its first out-of-London store.

When sumptuous, exclusive, designer-led surroundings become too much, the nearby Kirkgate Market (see page 60) offers a more down-to-earth alternative, albeit among the fine, ornate decoration of the **City Market Hall** (ⓐ Vicar Lane ⓦ www.leedsmarket.com). Anyone in search of retro/alternative clothing and accessories should head to either **Pop Boutique**

(ⓐ Central Road ⓦ www.pop-boutique.com) or the collection of independent shops along the rather tatty New York Street, Kirkgate and Call Lane. To the north, the **Merrion Centre** (ⓦ www.merrioncentre.co.uk), the **St Johns Centre** (ⓦ www.stjohnsleeds.co.uk), Briggate and The Headrow provide all the usual retail suspects.

TAKING A BREAK

Cafés & markets

Create Café £ ㉒ Located in the 19th-century Leeds Parish Church, this café delivers a little piece of affordable calm from the city bustle among its simple and wholesome décor, all lit by natural light streaming through the stained-glass windows. ⓐ St Peter's Church, Kirkgate ⓣ 0113 246 1659 ⓛ 10.00–16.00 Mon–Fri, 10.00–14.00 Sat, closed Sun

Kirkgate Market £ ㉓ Cheerful and cheap, there is a large selection of small stalls and huts in the market halls that hark back to a day when ordering a coffee was a simple affair (with milk and sugar or without). Serving hearty snacks and sandwiches, these cafés are so cosy that getting into conversation with strangers is often unavoidable. ⓐ Vicar Lane ⓦ www.leedsmarket.com ⓛ 09.00–17.00 Mon–Sat, closed Sun

Pickles and Potter £ ㉔ This popular deli and café set in the splendour of Queen's Arcade serves excellent sandwiches and light meals using locally sourced ingredients. ⓐ 18–20 Queen's Arcade ⓣ 0113 242 7702 ⓛ 09.00–17.00 Mon–Sat, 10.30–17.00 Sun

To revive yourself while shopping try Anthony's at Flannels

Anthony's at Flannels ££ ㉕ Upmarket loft-style café on the third floor of Flannels clothes store. The menu includes traditional British favourites prepared and presented with élan; hearty comforting lunches, sandwiches, light bites and elegant afternoon teas. ⓐ Flannels 3rd floor, 68 Vicar Lane ⓣ 0113 242 8732 ⓦ www.anthonysrestaurant.co.uk/flannels ⓛ 10.00–16.00 Tues–Sat, 10.30–16.00 Sun, closed Mon

Harvey Nichols Espresso Bar ££ ㉖ The breakfasts and traditional afternoon tea are good bets. ⓐ Briggate, Victoria Quarter ⓣ 0113 204 8000 ⓛ 10.00–18.00 Mon–Wed, 10.00–20.00 Thur, 10.00–19.00 Fri, 09.00–19.00 Sat, 10.00–17.00 Sun

Restaurants

Art's Café Bar & Restaurant £ ㉗ An enduringly bohemian Leeds institution for nearly 20 years, this bright, airy, simply furnished eatery brings cooking from the Mediterranean and Yorkshire together using local produce whenever possible. Look out for the work of local artists that regularly adorns its walls. ⓐ 42 Call Lane ⓣ 0113 243 8243 ⓦ www.artscafebar.com 🕒 12.00–23.00 Mon–Fri, 12.00–02.00 Sat, 10.30–23.00 Sun

Bibis ££ ㉘ Fantastically popular and vast Italian restaurant reputed to entertain over 4,000 customers a week. Kitsch with a capital K, its success and capacity makes for a noisy and crowded experience, especially when tribute acts take to the stage. Connoisseurs of fine Italian cooking will perhaps be a little perplexed by the crowds, but as an exercise in outlandish grandeur it's worth a visit. ⓐ Criterion Place, off Sovereign Street ⓣ 0113 243 0905 ⓦ www.bibisrestaurant.com 🕒 17.30–22.30 Mon–Thur, 17.30–23.00 Fri, 12.00–23.00 Sat, 12.00–22.00 Sun

Brasserie Forty 4 ££ ㉙ Bright and breezy waterside restaurant housed in a former grain warehouse and furnished in a contemporary style. When the weather is clement, there is a small balcony overlooking the river on which to enjoy the modern British/European fare. For those in need of a lift to and from the venue at lunchtimes, it offers a free chauffeur service around the city centre. ⓐ 44 The Calls ⓣ 0113 234 3232 ⓦ www.brasserie44.com 🕒 12.00–14.00 & 18.00–22.00 Mon–Fri, 13.00–15.00 & 17.00–22.00 Sat, closed Sun

Livebait ££ 30 Bright and jolly seafood restaurant tucked away from the bustle of the main shopping area. The menu is made up of a fantastic array of fish and shellfish dishes that all come with an ethical and sustainability guarantee and includes Canadian lobster, Devonshire crab, mussels and oysters. a 11–15 Wharf Street, Shears Yard, The Calls t 0113 244 4144 w www.livebaitrestaurants.co.uk 12.00–15.00 & 17.30–22.30 Mon–Thur, 12.00–23.00 Fri & Sat, closed Sun

River Plate ££ 31 Another eatery in The Calls that likes its girders and brickwork exposed. Though specialising in exquisitely prepared Argentinian beef, those less partial to the steaks will find a good choice of fish dishes. A narrow balcony offers alfresco drinking, dining and dreams of the Pampas during warm sunny days. a 36–38 The Calls t 0113 391 2792 w www.riverplate.co.uk 17.00–24.00 Mon–Sat, closed Sun

Anthony's £££ 32 A fun, unpretentious experience, this is food for food lovers but without the usual pomposity. a Trevelyan Square, off Boar Lane t 0113 245 5922 w www.anthonysrestaurant.co.uk 12.00–14.00 & 19.00–21.00 Tues–Thur, 12.00–14.00 & 19.00–22.00 Fri & Sat, closed Sun & Mon

AFTER DARK

Pubs & bars

Calls Landing £ 33 Exposed bricks and girders inside a terraced waterfront. Serving a vast range of beers and with a simple menu of stews, oysters and cheeses, this is a friendly, informal

The Victorian Quarter's huge stained-glass ceiling

hangout for local trendy types. ⓐ 36–38 The Calls ⓣ 0113 242 5299 ⓦ www.callslanding.com

Duck & Drake £ ㉞ Friendly, no-nonsense traditional real ale 'boozer', dedicated to regular live rock and blues music and located just a stone's throw from the trendy bars of The Calls. ⓐ 43 Kirkgate ⓣ 0113 245 5432 ⓦ www.duckndrake.co.uk

Oporto £ ㉟ One of the best-loved bars and live-music venues in the city attracts a mixed crowd to its minimalist yet stylish décor and ambience. ⓐ 33 Call Lane ⓣ 0113 243 4008 ⓦ http://oportobar.co.uk

Queens Court £ ㊱ The name is a bit of a giveaway. This small collection and cooperative of predominantly gay café-bars includes Queens Court itself, **The Loft** nightclub (ⓦ www.loftleeds.com) and **Bar Fibre** (ⓦ www.barfibre.com). During the summer and spring months they all come together for their famous courtyard parties. ⓐ 167–168 Lower Briggate ⓣ 0113 245 9449 ⓦ http://queenscourtleeds.com

Whitelocks £ ㊲ Tucked away down one of the city's many alleyways and described by John Betjeman as 'the very heart of Leeds', this is reputed to be the oldest pub in Leeds and is a celebration of old-world furnishings. A good range of ales and simple hearty food is served upstairs. Look out for the outside wall mural depicting the pub in a Yorkshire village scene under its original name. ⓐ Head Yard, Briggate ⓣ 0113 245 3950 ⓦ http://whitelocks.co.uk

Clubs & venues

The Birdcage £ 38 Raucously camp cabaret nightclub especially popular with hen nights and the gay community, featuring regular drag queens and showgirl performances every 30 minutes, with classic cheesy pop in between. Not for the faint-hearted or easily offended. Seats with table service can be booked in advance (t 0845 603 6950 ⏲ 10.00–19.00 Mon–Sat). a 52–56 Boar Lane t 0113 246 7273 w www.birdcagelive.com

The HiFi Club £ 39 This award-winning live music venue and nightclub features a diverse playlist and gig calendar. From soul to indie, jazz to comedy, the HiFi, despite its demure size, is one of the UK's most influential nightspots. a 2 Central Road t 0113 242 7353 w www.thehificlub.co.uk

Chilli White ££ 40 White furnishings, large gilt mirrors and Regency-style chairs set the scene in the main bar. Its upmarket name, cocktails and décor attract the well dressed, well-to-do and 'celebs' from far and wide to its regular themed nights over its three floors. a Assembly Street t 0113 219 4001 w www.chilliwhite.com

Outside the city centre

This area completely encircles the centre of the city. You will require transport to get to the outer reaches of the suburbs and the surrounding points of interest beyond. However, waterside attractions on the southern banks of the river – such as Clarence Dock and the Royal Armouries Museum – can be reached on foot from the city centre.

SIGHTS & ATTRACTIONS

Brewery Wharf

This new development of swish apartments, eating and drinking venues surround the 19th-century canal basin and make for a good alternative from the nearby city centre at night. As part of the waterside trail, this is also an interesting place to spend time during the day, getting to grips with how important water transport was to the city of Leeds. Ⓦ www.brewerywharf.net

Clarence Dock

Once used as a maritime distribution centre, this large basin is now home to a colourful collection of traditional narrow boats surrounded by modern blocks of retail, entertainment and living space. Look out for the inscribed paving slabs along the quayside relating its history. Ⓦ www.clarencedock.co.uk Bus: 28

Leeds Bridge

Historic access to the city across the River Aire, dating back to the medieval period when the city began its path to becoming

one of the world's most important textile trading towns. The current cast-iron incumbent dates from 1730 and is the location for the world's first-ever cinematic moving image (see box).
ⓐ Lower Briggate

Leeds City Cruisers
Offers a selection of cruises along the River Aire (including dinner and Sunday lunch excursions), as well as hourly river bus services over summer weekends and bank holidays, all aboard the purpose-built Black Prince. ⓐ Clarence Dock ⓣ 0845 388 4901 ⓦ www.leedscitycruisers.co.uk

THE BIRTH OF CINEMA
In 1888 a two-second film, shot from the upstairs window of an ironmonger's, recorded pedestrians, horses and carriages crossing Leeds Bridge. Generally considered to be the first-ever celluloid moving image, it was shot by inventor and photography enthusiast Louis Aimé Augustin Le Prince, who created cinematic history several years before the more famous and better-funded work of Georges Méliès, Thomas Edison and the Lumière brothers. However, with fortune and fame beckoning, Le Prince mysteriously disappeared while visiting his brother in France two years later and was never seen again. The cameras involved can now be seen at the National Media Museum in Bradford (see pages 71–2).

Roundhay Park

Vast open spaces, scented gardens, themed displays, woodland walks, lakes and fountains – and even its own castle gateway (albeit a Victorian folly) – make one of Europe's largest public parks a well-trodden urban escape for locals. Cafés are peppered throughout the park, as are numerous information boards and maps. ⓣ 0113 214 5715 ⓦ www.roundhaypark.org.uk Bus: 2, 12

Fountains in Roundhay Park

CULTURE

Harewood House

Art by Titian and J M W Turner, furniture by Chippendale and designs by Robert Adam, this magnificent home is packed to its 18th-century rafters with opulent treasures, all surrounded by landscaped gardens created by Capability Brown. A wide variety of events take place throughout the year, including exhibitions, craft displays and a host of themed events for the whole family. ⓐ Harewood ⓣ 0113 218 1010 ⓦ www.harewood.org ⓞ 10.30–16.00 daily ⓑ Bus: 36 (Service to Harewood village. A shuttle bus then connects the main gate with the house) ⓘ Admission charge

Kirkstall Abbey

Once home to 12th-century Cistercian monks, today Kirkstall remains one of the most complete examples of a medieval Cistercian abbey in the UK. As well as a fascinating attraction in its own right, there is an array of engaging and relaxing things to do here for all ages. The former gatehouse now houses a museum, which has at its heart re-created Victorian streets and an interactive childhood gallery. There is a children's miniature railway and a good spot for picnics by the river in the warmer months; it is also a summer venue for an array of outdoor concerts and theatrical productions. ⓐ Abbey Road, Kirkstall ⓣ 0113 230 5492 ⓦ www.leeds.gov.uk/kirkstallabbey ⓞ 11.00–16.00 Tues–Sun, closed Mon (Apr–Sept); 11.00–15.00 Tues–Thur, Sat & Sun, closed Mon & Fri (Oct–Mar) ⓑ 33, 33a, 757 ⓘ Admission charge to museum and events

A formidable cannon outside the Armouries

Leeds Industrial Museum

Just over 3 km (2 miles) from the city and once the largest woollen mill in the world, the museum now tells the fascinating tale of the city's manufacturing past in a child-friendly way, including spaces dedicated to clothing, printing, engineering and optics. ⓐ Armley Mills, Canal Road ⓣ 0113 263 7861 ⓦ www.leeds.gov.uk/armleymills 10.00–17.00 Tues–Sat, 13.00–17.00 Sun, closed Mon except open bank holidays 10.00–17.00 Bus: 5, 733, 734, 735, 736 Admission charge

National Media Museum

Spread over seven floors, Britain's foremost media attraction is packed with permanent and touring interactive exhibits, dedicated to the past, present and future of visual media.

It includes plenty of hands-on fun. There is also an IMAX cinema, tours, talks, gift shop and cafés. ⓐ Queensbury, Bradford ⓣ 0870 701 0200 ⓦ www.nationalmediamuseum.org.uk ◷ Galleries and shop 10.00–18.00 Tues–Sun, 10.00–18.00 Mon (school and bank holidays only); cinemas 10.00–late daily ⓝ Train: Bradford Interchange Station

Royal Armouries Museum

Tracing the history of arms and armour through the ages, this four-floor museum explores the art, technology and outcomes of militaria on the world through to the present day.

There are lots of interactive exhibits for children to get involved in, and the collection also includes a powerful gallery dedicated to weaponry perception and the devastating effects it has when in the hands of contemporary urban street gangs. Special events include outdoor falconry and horse shows, and suited-up jousting knights. ⓐ Clarence Road ⓣ 0113 220 1800 ⓦ www.royalarmouries.org ◷ 10.00–17.00 daily ⓝ Bus: 28

Saltaire Village & Mill

The original homes, shops and civic buildings of this 19th-century community remain a living, breathing and fascinating historical testament to the entrepreneurial visionary Titus Salt. Salt was a textile manufacturer who created a model village for his workers, away from the polluted centre of Bradford, with a church, a school and a park. It is now a World Heritage Site and the largest intact planned village in the UK. At its heart, Salts Mill (ⓣ 01274 531 163 ⓦ www.saltsmill.org.uk ◷ 10.00–17.30 daily) has been converted into a marvellous exhibition space

SALTAIRE – A MODEL FOR LIFE

The vision of one man, Saltaire is the largest and most intact planned village in the UK, a vast living memorial to the life, work and philanthropic philosophies of Titus Salt. Born in Leeds in 1803, Titus Salt later joined the family textile business and began to oversee five factories in nearby Bradford. Soon realising the horrific conditions and surroundings that workers endured, where cholera and typhoid were endemic, Salt was one of the few mill owners to show any concern for them. He was finally inspired to take his factory out of the polluted centre of Bradford to a nearby beauty spot on the banks of the River Aire – hence the name Saltaire.

Built between 1851 and 1876, no expense was spared on his vision. The Italianate façades of the factory hid a whole host of new devices and designs that would make the working conditions as tolerably safe and healthy as possible.

The village built for his workers was also made to be as pleasant and safe to inhabit as possible, with clean water supplies, plumbed lavatories and gas for heating and light. Public baths and wash-houses were provided to keep his workforce and their families clean from disease, and – driven by his charitable nonconformist background – a park, church, school, hospital and library were also commissioned.

Such was his commitment to public welfare that, despite the vast wealth he accumulated, most of his fortune was given away to good causes within his lifetime.

starring local boy David Hockney; it also houses three floors of eclectic shops and quirky cafés. ⓐ Saltaire, Shipley ⓦ www.saltairevillage.info Ⓝ Train: Saltaire Station

Thackray Museum

This is a fun, insightful and sometimes gory journey through the history of health and medicine in Leeds and the world beyond, which the whole family will enjoy. Housed in the former Leeds Union workhouse, there is a café on site. ⓐ Beckett Street ⓣ 0113 246 5350 ⓦ www.thackraymuseum.org ⓛ 10.00–17.00 daily Ⓝ Bus: 4, 42, 49, 50, 50A, 61 ⓘ Admission charge and car park fee

Salts Mill on the River Aire

Tropical World

Set within Roundhay Park, this manageable, child-friendly attraction features butterflies, meerkats, reptiles and equatorial plants among its warm and humid glasshouses and tanks. ⓐ Princes Avenue, Roundhay Park ⓣ 0113 214 5715 ◷ 10.30–17.30 daily (summer); 10.30–15.30 daily (winter) Bus: 2, 12 ❗ Admission charge

West Yorkshire Playhouse

One of the largest producing theatres in the UK, this acclaimed venue features new drama and touring productions. ⓐ Playhouse Square, Quarry Hill ⓣ 0113 213 7700 ⓦ www.wyp.org.uk Bus: Freecitybus

York Gate Gardens

Striking and charming in equal measure, this English garden oasis is noted for its architectural features and the wonderful views from its collection of contrasting themed and styled sections. ⓐ Back Church Lane, Adel ⓣ 0113 267 8240 ⓦ www.perennial.org.uk ◷ 14.00–17.00 Thur & Sun (Apr–Sept); 11.00–17.00 Sun & Mon (bank holiday weekends only) ❗ Admission charge

TAKING A BREAK

Cafés

Opposite Café £ ㊶ Popular hang-out in the university district, supplying academia with some of the best coffee, light snacks and cakes in the city. Interior wall space is given over to student artwork and the place is regularly awarded for its dedication to Fairtrade and organic Java. ⓐ 26 Blenheim Terrace, opposite Leeds University ⓣ 0113 243 1321 ⓦ www.oppositecafe.co.uk ⓛ 08.00–18.00 Mon–Fri, 09.00–17.00 Sat, closed Sun

Shaky Jakes £ 42 *Happy Days* revisited, this retro 50s milk bar features a bewildering array of fruit, confectionery and biscuit-based shakes. Try the Ferrero Rocher milkshake for an ambassadorial experience. ⓐ 15 North Lane, Headingley ⓣ 0113 217 9156 ⓦ www.shakyjakes.co.uk ⓛ 10.00–18.00 Mon–Wed, 10.00–20.00 Thur–Sat, 11.00–19.00 Sun

Restaurants

Kendells ££ 43 Excellent and extremely lively, Art Deco, Parisian-style bistro offering an eclectic and regularly changing seasonal menu (squirrel, anyone?). Rich in fowl and red meat, the main courses follow a good choice of traditional Gallic favourites. If there's room left, the desserts are worth the extra effort. Early bird menus are available and the service is informal and genuinely warm. ⓐ St Peter's Square ⓣ 0113 234 6553 ⓦ www.kendellsbistro.co.uk ⓛ 17.30–22.00 Mon–Sat, closed Sun

Mumtaz ££ 44 When only a curry will do and it has to be in grand surroundings, this colossally plush restaurant, decorated in the 20s style and overlooking Clarence Dock, will surely satisfy. Fit for royalty, its choice of splendid Kashmiri-inspired dishes and Indian staples, all finished off with some fine sweets, has even been endorsed by the Queen. ⓐ Clarence Dock

ⓣ 0113 242 4211 ⓦ www.mumtaz.co.uk ⓛ 12.00–24.00 daily
ⓝ Bus: 28

Olive Press ££ ㊺ Part of the well-regarded northern chain Heathcotes, this informal Italian eatery specialises in stone-baked pizza and is a popular spot for families. Set beside the tranquil waterfront, the modern furnishings complement the original 19th-century grain warehouse interiors. ⓐ Canal Wharf, Water Lane ⓣ 0113 244 6611 ⓦ www.heathcotes.co.uk ⓛ 11.30–22.00 Mon–Thur, 11.30–23.00 Fri & Sat, closed Sun

The Olive Tree ££ ㊻ Greek food is not that well represented in the city, but this lively, award-winning restaurant, set among the trendy eateries of Headingley, makes for a great Hellenic option. Early bird and student specials are available, along with a selection of meze sharing menus and established favourites. ⓐ 74–76 Otley Road, Headingley
ⓦ www.olivetreegreekrestaurant.co.uk ⓛ 18.00–22.00 Mon–Sat, 12.00–22.00 Sun

AFTER DARK

Pubs & bars

The Faversham £ ㊼ A student magnet because of its location, the 'Fav' has been part of the city's buzzing indie music scene for decades and features a host of gigs and events that run throughout the day and into the small hours. ⓐ 1–5 Springfield Mount ⓣ 0113 243 1481 ⓦ www.thefaversham.com
ⓛ 12.00–02.00 Mon–Sat, closed Sun

Don't Tell Titus ££ ⓼ Named with a knowing nod to Titus Salt (see box page 73), who, as a strict teetotaller, didn't touch the demon drink. This relaxed and friendly wine bar offers an array of food and drink over its comfortable and informal two floors. ⓐ 6 Victoria Road, Saltaire ⓣ 01274 595 633 ⓦ www.donttelltitus.co.uk ⓗ 10.00–24.00 daily

Casino

Alea ⓽ Large entertainment complex boasting opulent décor, dining and, of course, gaming. Featuring two elegant Indian and Mediterranean restaurants, five bars (live jazz Fri and Sat nights), and an array of gaming pursuits including poker tournaments (Fri–Wed). Free entry to over 18s only, no membership is required, though customers must be smartly dressed and bring photo ID. ⓐ 4 The Boulevard, Clarence Dock ⓣ 0113 341 3200 ⓦ www.aleacasinos.com ⓗ 12.00–06.00 daily ⓑ Bus: 28

Cinema

Hyde Park Picture House ⓾ Opened as a cinema in 1914, this is one of the few remaining examples of an Edwardian picture palace left in Britain, and a wonderful place to watch predominantly art-house releases surrounded by many of the building's original Grade-II-listed features. ⓐ 73 Brudenell Road, Headingley ⓣ 0113 275 2045 ⓦ www.hydeparkpicturehouse.co.uk ⓑ Bus: 56

A glorious sunset over Grassington, the Yorkshire Dales

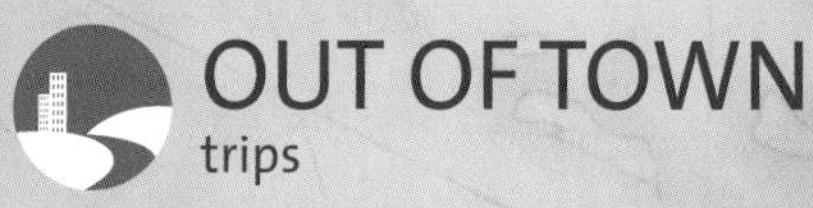
OUT OF TOWN
trips

Harrogate

The Victorians were the first to see the tourist potential of this pretty spa town and its endless supply of natural, health-giving water. Their eye for profit led to the vast building project to create the broad tree-lined streets, public gardens and handsome buildings that define Harrogate today. However, with most of the wells now closed, high-class retail, conferences and biannual flower shows (w www.flowershow.org.uk) have become the town's main attractions. Nearby Knaresborough has more of a village feel and does pack in some interesting pleasures for a town so small (w www.knaresborough.co.uk).

Getting to Harrogate from Leeds is a straightforward affair, either via a 35-minute train journey or by a bus ride of an hour or so (Bus: 36). Once there, the town is small enough to navigate on foot, though it is sited on quite a steep hill.

SIGHTS & ATTRACTIONS

Parks & gardens

A riot of colour and fragrance whatever the time of year, Harrogate really goes to town on its abundant public spaces and is a regular winner of the Britain in Bloom competition.

RHS Harlow Carr Gardens

A showcase setting for northern plants and flowers, alongside an array of glasshouses and distractions for children.
a Crag Lane, Harrogate t 01423 565 418
w www.rhs.org.uk/Gardens/Harlow-Carr 09.30–17.00 daily

(summer); 09.30–15.00 daily (winter) Bus: 6
Admission charge

Mother Shipton's Cave

This parkland amble culminates with a shallow cave and petrifying well said to have been inhabited by Mother Shipton, a 500-year-old prophetess, and features everyday calcified objects and a small museum. Prophecy Lodge, High Bridge 01423 864 600 www.mothershiptonscave.com 10.00–17.30 daily

Harrogate's Valley Gardens

(Apr–Oct); 10.00–16.30 Sat–Sun (Feb); 10.00–17.20 Sat & Sun (Mar) Train: Knaresborough Station (ten-minute walk) Admission charge

Royal Pump Room Museum

Housed in a former Victorian spa, this museum illustrates the history of Harrogate and also has a rolling programme of visiting exhibitions. It is possible to get a taste of the

Winter in Harrogate

quite revolting sulphurous waters, said to be the strongest in Europe. a Crown Place, Harrogate t 01423 556 188 w www.harrogate.gov.uk/harrogate-987 10.00–17.00 Mon–Sat, 14.00–17.00 Sun (summer); 10.00–17.00 Mon–Sat, 14.00–16.00 Sun (winter) ! Admission charge

Turkish Baths & Health Spa
One of England's last remaining Victorian Turkish baths certainly is an experience. Savour the atmosphere amid the ornate luxury, where pampering, relaxation and the occasional yelp are all part of the ritual. a Parliament Street, Harrogate t 01423 556 746 Open daily for female-only, male-only and mixed admissions; phone for details ! Admission charge

TAKING A BREAK

Bettys Café Tea Rooms ££ Phenomenal institution known for its fine collection of cakes and savouries, all served in a traditionally dainty English tea-shop atmosphere. Queuing is almost inevitable. a 1 Parliament Street, Harrogate t 01423 814 070 w www.bettys.co.uk 09.00–21.00 daily

AFTER DARK

Jakes £ Friendly and homely Italian café-bar serving flamboyant cakes and pastries during the day and locally sourced produce on its evening menus. a 47 Oxford Street, Harrogate t 01423 536 606 w www.jakeanthony.co.uk 09.00–17.30 Mon–Wed, 09.00–22.00 Thur–Sat, 10.00–17.00 Sun

Yorkshire Dales

An exceptional place of immense character and beauty, formed by nature and shaped by agriculture over thousands of years, the **Yorkshire Dales National Park** (ⓦ www.yorkshiredales.org.uk) is a breathtaking expanse of verdant meadows and heather moorland peppered with picturesque ancient villages such as Kettlewell, Grassington and Malham. Unique geographical features – caves, waterfalls, cliffs, natural limestone paths – attract walkers and thrill-seekers, while others are drawn simply by the beauty and tranquillity. The charming market town of Skipton is a good base and offers a host of places to shop and eat (ⓦ www.skiptononline.co.uk). It is also the largest and best-served gateway to the Dales, with a journey time of just 45 minutes from Leeds by train. This service continues northwards into the heart of the Dales along the stunning

A peaceful summer scene in Malham

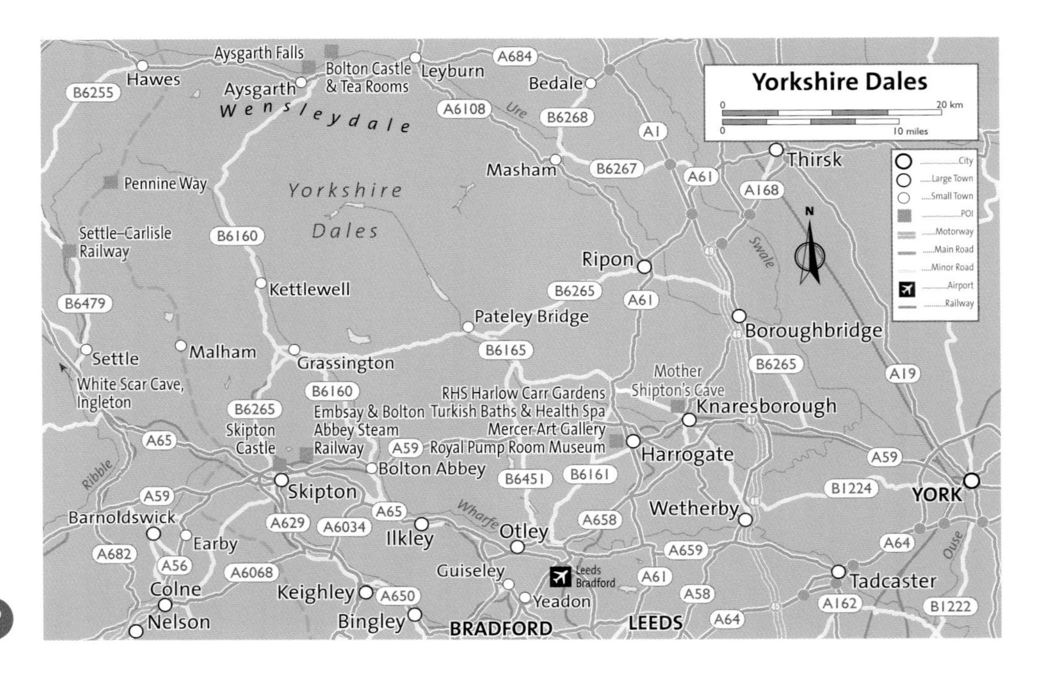
Yorkshire Dales
0
20 km
0
10 miles
City
Large Town
Small Town
POI
Motorway
Main Road
Minor Road
Airport
Railway
N
Aysgarth Falls
Bolton Castle & Tea Rooms
Leyburn
A684
Bedale
Hawes
B6255
Aysgarth
Wensleydale
A6108
Ure
B6268
A1
Thirsk
Masham
B6267
A61
A168
Pennine Way
Yorkshire Dales
Settle–Carlisle Railway
B6160
Swale
Ripon
Kettlewell
B6265
A61
B6479
Pateley Bridge
Boroughbridge
Settle
Malham
Grassington
B6165
B6265
A19
White Scar Cave, Ingleton
B6160
Mother Shipton's Cave
RHS Harlow Carr Gardens
Knaresborough
B6265
Embsay & Bolton Abbey Steam Railway
Turkish Baths & Health Spa
Mercer Art Gallery
Skipton Castle
A65
A59
Royal Pump Room Museum
Harrogate
A59
Bolton Abbey
B6451
B6161
Ribble
B1224
YORK
A59
Skipton
A65
Wharfe
Wetherby
Barnoldswick
A629
A6034
Ilkley
Otley
A658
A64
Earby
A682
A659
Ouse
A56
A6068
Guiseley
Leeds Bradford
A61
Tadcaster
Colne
Keighley
A650
A58
A162
B1222
Yeadon
Nelson
Bingley
BRADFORD
LEEDS
A64

Aysgarth Falls

Settle to Carlisle railway (w www.settle-carlisle.co.uk). For bus travel, go to w www.dalesbus.org

SIGHTS & ATTRACTIONS

Aysgarth Falls

Set among ancient woodland, the falls offer a dramatic spot for picnickers and paddlers alongside an information centre and café. t 01969 662 910 10.00–17.00 daily (Apr–Oct); 10.00–16.00 Fri–Mon (Nov, Dec, Feb & Mar)

Embsay & Bolton Abbey Steam Railway

Chuffing through glorious scenery, go back in time along this heritage railway. a Railway Station, Bolton Abbey t 01756 710 614 w www.embsayboltonabbeyrailway.org.uk Weekends & selected weekdays (Apr–Dec) ! Admission charge for travel

Skipton Castle

This 900-year-old fortress is well preserved. a High Street t 01756 792 442 w www.skiptoncastle.co.uk 10.00–18.00 Mon–Sat, 12.00–18.00 Sun (Mar–Sept); 10.00–16.00 Mon–Sat, 12.00–16.00 Sun (Oct–Feb) ! Admission charge

White Scar Cave

Invigorating 80-minute guided descent into bedrock to see waterfalls, caverns and stalactites. Flat shoes and warm clothing recommended. a Ingleton t 01524 241 244 w www.whitescarcave.co.uk 10.00–16.00 daily (Feb–Oct); 10.00–16.00 Sat & Sun (Nov–Jan) ! Admission charge

A DRAMATIC BACKDROP

Aysgarth Falls has been immortalised in words, paint and celluloid for the past two centuries. William Wordsworth wrote of his visit there in 1812, J M W Turner captured it in oil – and more recently Robin Hood (aka Kevin Costner) took on Little John on the upper reaches of the falls in the film *Robin Hood: Prince of Thieves*. The triple flight of falls extends over a 1.6-km (1-mile) stretch of the River Ure, the water cascading down the valley as it descends to Wensleydale over a series of broad limestone steps.

TAKING A BREAK

Town End Farm Tearoom £ Café featuring seasonal fare together with a shop space selling produce from the farm next door and a gift shop, all situated close to the popular hiking village of Malham. ⓐ Airton, Skipton ⓣ 01729 830 902 ⓦ www.townendfarmshop.co.uk ⓛ 10.00–17.00 Tues–Sun, closed Mon

Vennells £££ On the eastern boundary of the National Park, this family-run restaurant excels in classic British food, cooked and served with real panache. ⓐ 7 Silver Street, Masham ⓣ 01765 689 000 ⓦ www.vennellsrestaurant.co.uk ⓛ 19.15–23.30 Tues–Sat, 12.30–14.00 Sun, closed Mon

Signs pointing the way

PRACTICAL information

Directory

GETTING THERE

By air

Just a short road journey from the city centre, 'no frills' airlines dominate the apron of Leeds Bradford Airport (LBA) (t 0871 288 2288 w www.leedsbradfordairport.co.uk e customerservices@lbia.co.uk) with Jet2 (w www.jet2.com), Ryanair (w www.ryanair.com) and Flybe (w www.flybe.com) particularly well represented.

Many people are aware that air travel emits CO_2, which contributes to climate change. You may be interested in the possibility of lessening the environmental impact of your flight through the charity **Climate Care** (w www.jpmorganclimatecare.com), which offsets your CO_2 by funding environmental projects around the world.

By rail

There are regular services across the UK to its major towns and cities, with frequent express trains from London King's Cross to Leeds in just over two hours. Contact National Rail. t 0845 748 4950 w www.nationalrail.co.uk

By road

In the centre of England and sitting at the crossroads of the M1 and M62 motorways, Leeds is easy to reach. Once there, the A64 and A58 inner ring roads lead traffic into the city's clockwise one-way system. National coaches arrive into the Leeds Bus and Coach Station, and travel, including the 4½-hour journey from

London, is provided by National Express. ⓣ 0871 781 8178 ⓦ www.nationalexpress.com

By ferry

Leeds is almost equidistant (a journey time of around 90 minutes by road) from the ports of Liverpool (for services to the Irish Republic) and Hull (for crossings to mainland Europe). Both are served by P&O Ferries. ⓦ www.poferries.com

Those travelling from Belfast, also via Liverpool, should contact Norfolk Line. ⓣ 0844 847 5042 ⓦ www.norfolkline.com

HEALTH, SAFETY & CRIME

Crime is unfortunately a global phenomenon and Leeds fares no better or worse than any other British city. Streetwise precautions should always be employed, including keeping expensive cameras and phones tucked away and closely shielding ATM number pads from prying eyes when withdrawing money. Don't let inebriated companions go wandering off alone into the city streets in the middle of the night – put them in a taxi first. It's also worth pocketing your hotel's business card before a night out so it can be shown to taxi drivers in case you get lost.

If there is a crime in progress or danger to life requiring police, fire or ambulance, phone ⓣ 999. For non-emergencies, phone West Yorkshire Police ⓣ 0845 606 0606.

MEDICAL SERVICES

Late-night pharmacy Boots ⓐ Public concourse, Leeds Station ⓣ 0113 242 1713 ⓑ 06.00–24.00 Mon–Fri, 08.00–24.00 Sat, 09.00–24.00 Sun

The Leeds General Infirmary ⓣ 0113 243 2799
NHS Walk-In Centre ⓐ The Light, The Headrow ⓣ 0870 818 0003
ⓛ 07.00–19.00 Mon–Fri
Leeds Dental Advice Line ⓣ 0800 298 5787 ⓛ 09.00–17.00
Mon–Fri (Out of hours ⓣ 0345 605 9999)

OPENING HOURS

On the whole, most high street shops open between 09.00 and 17.30 Monday to Saturday, and between 11.00 and 16.00 on Sunday. Smaller convenience stores are often open from dawn until the wee small hours. All banks are open between 09.30 and 16.30 Monday to Friday, with many also offering their services on Saturday morning.

TOILETS

Leeds City Train Station has pay toilets in the main concourse for non-travelling users and free facilities on the platforms beyond the ticket barriers. Free-to-use public toilets with disabled and baby-changing facilities can also be found in The Light retail/entertainment complex, Kirkgate Market and in the Leeds Art Gallery and City Museum.

CHILDREN

A vast area of the city centre is given over to pedestrian traffic, making it particularly safe and manageable for those travelling with children. For those with prams and pushchairs, most buildings in Leeds have access ramps and lifts within. Head to Leeds City Museum (see pages 47–8) for stuffed animals and interactive cultural displays, or to the sobering yet engaging Royal

Armouries Museum (see page 72) for some child-friendly educational fun. If children simply want to let off some steam, take them to Roundhay Park, where they'll find acres of green space, playgrounds and the live animals, insects and birds of the Tropical World that should engage all ages (see pages 69, 75).

TRAVELLERS WITH DISABILITIES

The city centre is on a gentle gradient, but the large pedestrianised zone that encompasses the bulk of retail Leeds makes getting around without road crossings fairly stress-free. All new buildings are required by law to provide disability access facilities, while those built in a previous era have incorporated lifts and ramps into existing structures. The Freecitybus that regularly circles the centre is also designed to be disability friendly.

Visitors can take advantage of the Shopmobility scheme, which offers rental services on all kinds of equipment, including wheelchairs and scooters. ⓐ Unit 92, Merrion Centre ⓣ 0113 246 0125 ⓦ www.shopmobilityuk.org ⓛ 09.30–16.30 Mon–Sat, closed Sun ⓑ Bus: Freecitybus; Woodhouse Lane

FURTHER INFORMATION

Leeds Visitor Centre

ⓐ Leeds Visitor Centre, Leeds City Train Station ⓣ 0113 242 5242 ⓦ www.visitleeds.co.uk ⓛ Daily

Another very useful website is ⓦ www.yorkshire.com

M

N

O

P

Q

R

S

T

V

W

X

Y

ACKNOWLEDGEMENTS
The photographs in this book were taken by Paul Cooper and Kathryn West for Thomas Cook Publishing, to whom the copyright belongs, except for the following: iStockphoto page 11 (Paul Wilkinson), page 16 (Gary Dyson), pages 39, 41 (Kelvin Jay), page 52 (Rob Ford), page 82 (Mikeuk), page 84 (Charlie Bishop); Shutterstock page 69 (Broad Acre Media), page 74 (Gyrohype), page 79 (Steve Smith), page 81 (David Peta), page 86 (Stephen Meese).

Project editor: Thomas Willsher
Copy editor: Penny Isaac
Proofreaders: Karolin Thomas & Caroline Hunt
Layout: Julie Crane
Indexer: Penelope Kent

AUTHOR BIOGRAPHY
A member of the British Guild of Travel Writers and published throughout the world, freelance travel writer and broadcaster David Cawley is a card-carrying northerner specialising in UK destinations. A regular visitor to the city, David is a keen advocate of all things Leeds and Yorkshire.

Send your thoughts to
books@thomascook.com

- **Found a great bar, club, shop or must-see sight that we don't feature?**
- **Like to tip us off about any information that needs a little updating?**
- **Want to tell us what you love about this handy little guidebook and more importantly how we can make it even handier?**

Then here's your chance to tell all! Send us ideas, discoveries and recommendations today and then look out for your valuable input in the next edition of this title.

Email the above address (stating the title) or write to:
pocket guides Series Editor, Thomas Cook Publishing, PO Box 227, Coningsby Road, Peterborough PE3 8SB, UK.